COLLECTED

POEMS

Books by Louis Jenkins

The Well Digger's Wife

The Wrong Tree

The Water's Easy Reach

An Almost Human Gesture

All Tangled Up with the Living

Nice Fish: New and Selected Prose Poems

Just Above Water

The Winter Road

Sea Smoke

Distance from the Sun

Four Places on Lake Superior's North Shore

Fisk på tørt land, prosadikt

European Shoes

North of the Cities

Before You Know It

Tin Flag

In the Sun Out of the Wind

Where Your House Is Now

The Mad Moonlight

By Louis Jenkins and Richard C. Johnson

Words and Pictures

By Mark Rylance and Louis Jenkins

Nice Fish: A Play

COLLECTED

POEMS

Louis Jenkins

Will o' the Wisp Books

ISBN: 978-0-9793128-9-2

Cover portrait: Laure Dosso

Will o' the Wisp Books
5521 Auto Club Road
Bloomington, MN 55437

willothewispbooks.com

for family, steadfast friends,
and interested readers

CONTENTS

from **An Almost Human Gesture** – 1987

from **All Tangled Up with the Living** – 1991

from **Nice Fish** – 1995

from **Just Above Water** – 1997

from **The Winter Road** – 2000

from **Sea Smoke** – 2004

from Distance from the Sun – 2004

from North of the Cities – 2007

from **North of the Cities (continued)**

from **European Shoes – 2008**

from **Words and Pictures – 2012**

from Tin Flag – 2008

from In the Sun Out of the Wind – 2017

from **Where Your House Is Now** – 2019

from **The Mad Moonlight** – 2019

PREFACE

It is with love and admiration that we put together this collection of my husband Louis Jenkins' poems and miscellaneous writings, with many thanks to the University of Minnesota's Upper Midwest Literary Archives, which houses the Jenkins papers. The collection of papers and ephemera there includes the early notebooks in which Jenkins usually started poems and left notes to himself about possible ideas to pursue. But, as he was an early user of the computer for writing, the content of the notebooks tapers off rapidly at some time in the 1980s or 1990s.

This book contains the published poems, but also includes some early drafts and notes that seem worthy of sharing in the last section, "Fragments from the Notebooks, Unpublished Poems and Early Drafts." He did publish work in many periodicals and anthologies, but we did not attempt to locate and include them, as most do appear in his books eventually. The arrangement of this collection is chronological for the most part. As several of the books contain "selected poems" as well as new work, the individual poems will only appear here once, with their first publication.

Louis Jenkins' life was entirely devoted to his writing. Although he held a variety of jobs, he chose not to pursue an academic career. He worked in libraries, painted houses, was a commercial fisherman on Lake Superior, a bread dough mixer, an oil fieldworker in Oklahoma, and a museum guard, but the poems were always on his mind. His method of writing was to get an idea, jot it down in a notebook or on a scrap of paper, and then think about and refine the words. Finally, when he had it almost perfect, he would sit down at the keyboard and type it out. Then he would work until he was satisfied with how it looked on the page. He was very careful about the format on the printed page. It had to look just right, especially the prose poems.

In addition to the poems and prose pieces, Jenkins collaborated with Mark Rylance in writing (and briefly acting in) a play, *Nice Fish*. It was the brainchild of Mark, who wanted to use Louis' poems as dialogue. It had successful runs at the Guthrie Theater in Minneapolis, the American Repertory Theater in Cambridge, St. Ann's Warehouse in Brooklyn, and the Harold Pinter Theater in London.

It's a gift to have a lifelong mission. Louis Jenkins had that gift. Writing successful poems was his raison d'être.

He was influenced by many fellow writers, mentors, and poets, including Robert Bly, Wallace Stevens, Robert Frost, Elizabeth Bishop, Russell Edson, Charles Simic, James Tate, Charles Baudelaire, Jean Follain, Max Jacob, Francis Ponge, Daniel Kharms, and Zbigniew Herbert, to name just a few.

We owe many thanks to all of his colleagues and friends, especially to Mark Rylance, Michael VanWalleghen, Michael Dennis Browne, Jean Jacobson, Phil Dentinger, Connie Wanek, Bart Sutter, Garrison Keillor, Joyce Sutphen, Freya Manfred, and Dianne Mathis, all of whom contributed to his rich and well-lived life. With special thanks to John Toren for helping design and put together this book, and to Lyle Koivisto for financial support and encouragement.

Ann Jenkins

A Few Words About
the Prose Poem

It was the freedom of the prose poem which first attracted me, its flexibility which makes it hospitable to images from the unconscious and to conscious narrative, which allows language that is lyrical to coexist with that which is prosaic. I loved the idea of a poem that worked without rhyme, meter or predetermined line breaks, things which insist that the reader should be having a poetic experience. Yet in some ways the prose poem seems to me to be a very formal poem.

The form of the prose poem is the rectangle, one of our most useful geometric shapes. Think of the prose poem as a box, perhaps the lunch box Dad brought home from work at night. What's inside? Some waxed paper, a banana peel, half a peanut butter-jelly sandwich. Not so much, a hint of how the day has gone perhaps, but magic for having made a mysterious journey and returned. The dried out pb&j tastier than anything made fresh.

The prose poem is a formal poem because of its limits. The box is made for travel, quick and light. Think of the prose rectangle as a small suitcase. One must pack carefully, only the essentials, too much and the reader won't get off the ground. Too much and the poem becomes a story, a novel, an essay or worse. The trick in writing a prose poem is discovering how much is enough and how much is too much. We know that a sonnet has fourteen lines but the prose poem is a formal poem with unspecified limits. Here is part of a prose poem by Tomas Transtromer:

> *I am welcomed aboard a boat—it's a canoe hollowed from a dark tree. The canoe is incredibly rocky, even when you sit on your heels. A balancing act. If you have the heart on the left side you have to lean a bit to the right, nothing in the pockets, n big arm movements, please, all rhetoric has to be left behind. It's necessary: rhetoric will ruin everything here. The canoe glides over the water.*

> (from "Standing Up"
> translated from the Swedish by Robert Bly)

The prose poems in this book [*Nice Fish: New and Selected Prose Poems*} were chosen from those I have written over the past twenty-five years. During that time I thought very little about the prose poem form. I simply tried to write as well as I could. Whatever craft I gained, what few ideas I got about form, came from that process. The prose poem is more than the luggage it is also the journey. Think of the prose poem as a door, another useful rectangle.

THE DELIGHTS OF THE DOOR

Kings don't touch doors.

They don't know this joy: to push affectionately or fiercely before us one of those huge panels we know so well, then to turn back in order to replace it—holding a door in ourarms. The pleasure of grabbing one of those tall barriers to a room abdominally, by its porcelain knot; of this swift fighting, body-to-body, when, the forward motion for an instant halted, the eye opens and the whole body adjusts to its new surroundings.

But the body still keeps one friendly hand on the door, holding it open, then decisively pushes the door away, closing itself in—which the click of the powerful but well-oiled spring pleasantly confirms.

(by Francis Ponge,
translated from the French by Robert Bly)

Louis Jenkins, 1995

COLLECTED

POEMS

The Well Digger's Wife

1973

THE PLAGIARIST

A fat teaching assistant has caught a freshman cheating on his exam and she stands now in the hallway displaying the evidence, telling the story to her colleagues: "I could tell by the way he looked. I could tell by his hands." With each detail the story expands, rooms are added, hallways, chandeliers, flights of stairs, and she sinks exhausted against a railing. More listeners arrive and she begins again. She seems thinner now, lighter. She rises, turns. She seems almost to be dancing. She clutches the paper of the wretched student. He holds her firmly, gently as they turn and turn across the marble floor. The lords and ladies fall back to watch as they move toward the balcony and the summer night. Below in the courtyard soldiers assemble, their brass and steel shining in the moonlight.

THE WELL DIGGER'S WIFE

I've been thinking of mountains on these hot nights, or better yet, the window ledge high above the bed and this tangle of sheets. It must be cool there with the breeze from the open window, and clean, painted white, like snow, only not so cold or wet. And not so steep as a mountaintop, like a great plain stretching out for miles. I started to move there once, last summer, taking just a few things I'd need: the cat, the mirror, a hatful of needles. But then he came home and caught me, broke two of my ribs and put an ugly bruise on my cheek. Every day now the sound of digging grows more faint. The sound of boots slogging through the mud is gone and the rocks roll away miles below me.

JANUARY NIGHT 35 BELOW ZERO

It is no longer fun
to burrow into my covers
as I did when I was a child
pretending to be a rabbit or a fox.
Tonight I will say my prayer
to whatever small creature is moving
in the woods beyond my window
so fierce in its life.

FEVER

I am being interviewed
for the job of Area Representative.
I am flying over the tundra at 250 mph,
my nose and fingertips not more than three inches
        above the ice.

I wake to discover that the glasses and bottles
on the table by the bed have crowded together,
waiting to be taken across the river.

When I fall asleep again I dream
that a pen with an extremely fine point
is signing on a tiny scrap of paper
my name over and over again.
It is all perfectly clear.

I have never really noticed the things in this room.
I have been unaware of their articulations:
the longings of the chest,
the desires of the bed,
the faint groaning of the walls at night,
those obscure concessions the house makes to the earth,
        settling.

The room is quiet now,
everything falling at the same rate of speed.

MY FEET

When I awake and look at my feet
I realize they must have waited all night,
immigrants clutching their papers,
clumsy thick-bodied peasants
still heavy with the old soil.
I think how many days they
must have stared at the ocean in dismay,
tried to cling to the pitch and roll,
no talent for swimming.
Now they stand, weary, bewildered,
still waiting, wondering which steps
to take across the snows
of this first long winter
in the new world.

IOWA

In Iowa the land is gently rolling, the towns are small but there seem to be a great many of them. In Iowa the farms are closer together than in Kansas or Nebraska and the barns and houses more neatly painted, red and white.

I have fallen asleep in Iowa and awakened to darkness everywhere dotted with small blue-white lights.

Iowa is primarily an agricultural state, one of the nation's largest producers of corn and pigs. Iowa is also the home of the world famous Writers' Workshop, one of the nation's largest producers of poets.

When looking at a map of Iowa it does not appear to be a very large state, but I have ridden a bus through Iowa and discovered it to be quite lengthy, its northern border running through the heart of Minneapolis.

MY FATHER

My father has a head for figures.
He knows how much it costs to build something
or repair it. He can estimate how high, how deep.
He knows how far away it is and how
many coats of paint it would take to cover.

I am his son, but I can only remember words:
I'm hungry ... I'm tired ... Why? ...
and small sounds:
a sigh,
a shadow slumping into a chair,
the click of a light turned out.

BASKETBALL

A huge summer afternoon with no sign of rain ... Elm trees in the farmyard bend and creak in the wind. The leaves are dry and gray. In the driveway a boy shoots a basketball at a goal above the garage door. Wind makes shooting difficult and time after time he chases the loose ball. He shoots, rebounds, turns, shoots ... on into the afternoon. In the silence between the gusts of wind the only sounds are the thump of the ball on the ground and the rattle of the bare steel rim of the goal. The gate bangs in the wind, the dog in the yard yawns, stretches and goes back to sleep. A film of dust covers the water in the trough. Great clouds of dust rise from open fields that stretch a thousand miles beyond the horizon.

DOING NOTHING

On a warm day Phil and I go down to the lakeshore, sit on the rocks at the water's edge and drink beer. There is a cool breeze blowing off Lake Superior and a few cirrus clouds high above. As we talk a cedar waxwing comes toward us, hopping from stone to stone. He comes very near and stops. He cocks his head to listen and look at us. We are too heavy, our wings are useless, and we can see in only one direction at a time. He gives up and flies away. The rock I am sitting on is huge and round with a fringe of moss, like hair, around the edge just below the waterline. It is like sitting atop a monk's head. I reach down and the cold water surges up to touch my hand. It occurs to me that we are underway and I have no idea how to pilot this thing.

KANSAS

As she smells the clean sheets the farmer's wife thinks of the 1930s. Wind whips the clothes on the line, blows her dress tight against her heavy legs.

The farmer in his dirty overalls searches through years of broken machinery behind the barn, searches through tall sunflowers, through the nests of rabbits and mice with a wrench in his hand, looking for exactly the right part or one that might do.

Seven skinny cows lie in the mud where the tank overflows. Throughout the long afternoon the windmill continues to pump long draughts of cool water.

SKILLET

The skillet is heavy and black, too heavy to carry on a long hike, but completely functional. The skillet has lived a life of service, worked hard. The skillet will not accept charity.

The skillet's mouth is always open as if it were trying to tell me something of fire, of darkness and poverty but manages only to sputter platitudes of protestant virtue.

Still, I believe the skillet has some understanding of its life. For a few moments each morning when I fry eggs the skillet opens its large eyes and stares intently at me and at the fork in my hand.

SELF-SERVICE LAUNDRY

I'm done with canned coke,
cellophane packaged peanuts,
movie magazines with missing pages
revealing the truth about the death of Marilyn Monroe.
The attendant has emptied the ash trays and gone home
and I'm ready but the machines
continue in their crazy orbit.
If I rub the condensation from the window
I can see across the street,
the railroad tracks and the ice cream store and beyond,
the trees, the night where it begins,
as I am hurled past.

THE LAKE

Streets run straight downhill to the water. The lake brings the city to an end. It is there, always, changing the direction of my walks. Sometimes I go for days without coming near, catching only a glimpse through the trees, a sail, a white speck turning on the dark blue. Perhaps someone very old touched the back of my wrist, lightly, for only the briefest moment, or you said something to me. What was it? The waters close above my head suddenly without a sound.

FISHING BELOW THE DAM

On summer evenings the workingmen gather to fish in the swift water below the dam. They sit on the rocks and are silent for the most part, looking into the water and casting again and again. Lines tangle, tackle is lost and a fisherman curses to himself. No one notices. It is simply a part of the routine, like the backs of their wives in bed at night or short words to the children in the morning. Only the water holds their attention, crashing through the spillway with enough force behind it to break a man's back. And the undertow could take you as easily as a bit of fish line and toss you ashore miles downstream. The men shout to be heard above the roar of the water. ANY LUCK? NO I JUST GOT HERE.

YOU MOVE A CHAIR

You move a chair from its place in the corner
and suddenly you realize
someone had been sitting there all along.
You start to apologize.
Oh, no bother, he says and jumps up.
You are embarrassed, anxious.
He stands at the window,
hands folded behind his back,
watching the snow drift into the yard.
You can't think of anything to say.
You begin to hum in a nervous monotone.
You stand by the door.
Finally you try replacing the chair
but it's no use.
When you turn again he'll be gone.

STORM

The storm begins with the wind. After centuries of settled life the trees become nomads. The message passes throughout the camp. Horses and dogs grow restless. The tribe prepares to move away during the night.

Lightning strikes very near and the electricity goes dead. The clock stops. The voice on the radio fades. We sit huddled in the dark living room as in a cave, without light, without words.

The first drops of rain striking the roof make a wooden sound: mice scurrying over the rafters or a handful of dirt thrown on a coffin.

The rain continues to fall all night. We sleep and drift among roads, houses and people we have known. I wake and listen: the sound of rain, the sound of our breathing. Water rising.

BARBER SHOP

Someone is helping an old man into the barber shop. The old man is neatly dressed in a blue pinstripe suit that might have been purchased sometime during the Second World War, perhaps for a funeral. He seems unaware of his clothes or his surroundings. Perhaps someone else chose the suit and the clean white shirt and dressed him as one would dress a large doll. He seems to enjoy the warm afternoon sun and seems reluctant to enter the shop. The sun glints on water and steel, on the windows, on scissors and shears and on his great shock of white hair. The voices he hears change and change and he recognizes none of them. The sound of his own name is like a door opening into a dark room—the momentary glare when someone wearing soft-soled shoes enters and leaves again.

DURING THE NIGHT

Sometime during the night we are called for a conference on the shooting of the final scenes. In one version I am the honest grocer constantly sweeping the front porch in front of the general store, an eye peeled for outlaws, longing for my other life and the Colt .44's in a box behind the counter. There are other stories. In the one just before I wake up I am drunk and nearly blind, my feet troubled by all manner of small objects. I manage finally to stumble down to the tracks. The light comes rushing down upon me.

THE POET

He is young and thin with dark hair and a deep, serious voice. He sips his coffee and says, "I have found that it is a good idea to check the words you use in a dictionary. I keep a list. Here is the word *meadow*. Since I was a child the word *meadow* always had connotations of peace and beauty. Once I used *meadow* in a poem and as a matter of practice I looked the word up. I found that a *meadow* was a small piece of grassland used to graze animals ... Somehow *meadow* was no longer a thing of beauty..."

It is spring. A few cows are grazing in the muddy meadow. There are patches of blackened snow beside the road. It is nearly dark and the ragged poplars at the far end of the meadow have turned black. The animals, the stones, the grass, everything near the earth darkens, and above: the *azure sky*.

INTERMISSION

The violins have gone; the brass and woodwinds have gone. The orchestra has just finished a Paganini concerto. The basses and cellos lie on the floor or recline against chairs, weary and unimpressed. They are like soldiers or prisoners on a ten-minute break and no one has any cigarettes. In a far corner, dressed in black, the drummer hunches over the tympani like a raven picking over a rabbit killed on the highway or like an old woman bending over a kettle brewing a poison to be painted on telephone poles to kill all the woodpeckers. He tunes and tests the drum. He puts his ear close. What does he hear? A distant storm? A herd of buffalo? Perhaps railroad crews working hard to lay down track a few miles ahead of a locomotive, the cars richly furnished with carpet, crystal and fine wine. The beautiful ladies and gentlemen come laughing and talking down the aisles to find their seats.

The Wrong Tree

1980

FOOTBALL

I take the snap from center, fake to the right, fade back, I've got protection. I've got a receiver open downfield... What the hell is this? This isn't a football, it's a shoe, a man's brown leather oxford. A cousin to a football maybe, the same skin, but not the same, a thing made for the earth, not the air. I realize that this is a world where anything is possible and I understand, also, that one often has to make do with what one has. I have eaten pancakes, for instance, with that clear corn syrup on them because there was no maple syrup and they weren't very good. Well, anyway, this is different. (My man downfield is waving his arms.) One has certain responsibilities, one has to make choices. This isn't right and I'm not going to throw it.

VIOLENCE ON TELEVISION

It is best to turn on the set only after all the stations have gone off the air and just watch the snowfall. This is the other life you have been promising yourself; somewhere back in the woods, ten miles from the nearest town, and that just a wide place in the road with a tavern and a gas station. When you drive home, after midnight, half drunk, the roads are treacherous. And your wife is home alone, worried, looking anxiously out at the snow. This snow has been falling steadily for days, so steadily the snowplows can't keep up. So you drive slowly, peering down the road. And there! Did you see it? Just at the edge of your headlight beams, something, a large animal, or a man, crossed the road. Stop. There he is among the birches, a tall man wearing a white suit. No, it isn't a man. Whatever it is it motions to you, an almost human gesture, then retreats farther into the woods. He stops and motions again. The snow is piling up all around the car. Are you coming?

MOTORCYCLE

He climbs on, switches on the ignition, kicks the starter: once, twice, three, four, five times…Nothing. He tries a dozen more times. It won't go. He checks the gas tank. Got gas. He switches the key off and on, tries again. It still won't go. He climbs off the bike and squats down to look at the engine. Check the carburetor, check the wires … seems okay. He takes a wrench from his jacket pocket and removes the spark plug. He examines it, blows on it, wipes it on his jeans, replaces the plug, climbs back on the bike and tries again. Nothing. Now he is getting really angry. There is absolutely no reason why this thing shouldn't start. He gets off the bike and stands and stares at it. He gets back on and kicks the starter really hard half-a-dozen times. Now he is furious. He gets off and throws the wrench he is still holding as far as he can. It bounces on the gravel down the road and skids into the weeds in the ditch. Then he turns and kicks the son-of-a-bitch motorcycle over on its side and walks away. After a short distance he thinks better of it and returns to the motorcycle. It isn't sobbing quietly. It doesn't say, "I don't want to play with you anymore," or "I don't love you anymore," or "I have my own life to live," or "I have the children to think of." It only lies there leaking oil and gas. He rights the motorcycle and carefully wipes off the dust, carefully mounts and once more tries the starter. Even now it won't go. He gets down and sits in the dirt beside the broken motorcycle.

A DRIVE IN THE COUNTRY
ON THE FIRST FALL DAY

Everything pleases me. I like the way the sun shines on the farm house, on the tin cans and broken bottles in the junk pile, on the cretin teenage boy standing in the driveway. I like the way the popple trees come right up to the farmyard and stop.

It has been a warm summer. Now all signs point to a long cold winter. For instance, the farmer has laid in an extra supply of wood for his stove. I like the way the sun shines on the white split logs.

ASLEEP AT THE WHEEL

He falls asleep at the wheel and dreams that everything
is the same; he is still driving at night through the long
pine forest. Mile after mile glides through the automobile.
He manages distances more easily now so there is time
to discern in the night forest a single tree, a stone, or a
hidden path. These things seem as familiar and absorbing
as a love affair or his own childhood. He sees for the
first time that the forest extends not fifty or a hundred
miles, but infinitely on either side of the road, and that it
is possible to wander there forever, alone, and not die ...
The car veers into the gravel at the edge of the blacktop.
He wrenches the wheel back to the left. He is wide-awake.
The car is on the road, speeding toward the end of its
headlight beams.

DRIFTWOOD

It is pleasant to lie on the rocky shore in the sun, exposed and open. It's all there; the sound of wind, the sound of waves, the meaningless journal of a lifetime. Nothing is clear, not even the obvious. One loses interest and falls asleep within the water's easy reach.

This driftwood on the beach, dry and bleached white, white as a bone you might say, or white as snow. If an artist (wearing a sweatshirt, blue jeans and tennis shoes without socks) came walking along he might, seeing the possibilities, pick up this piece of driftwood and take it home. Not me. I fling it back in the water.

LIFE IS SO COMPLEX

Life is so complex, even though you eat brown rice and brush your teeth with baking soda. Simplify. Spend the day alone. Spend it fishing. Watch the line and the motion of the water; your thoughts drift ... a slight bump and a steady pull on the line and the whole line of cars begins to move as the train pulls out of the station. Someone takes the seat beside you, someone at the end of a love affair. The threats of murder and suicide, the pleading, the practical jokes, became at the end only tiresome and she is relieved at his going. She turns away before the train is out of sight.

Your ordinary life is simple, full of promise, bullet-like, pushing aside the waves of air, moving with incredible speed toward the life that waits, motionless, unsuspecting, at the heart of the forest.

A POOL GAME

They share a cuestick. He breaks, makes the four ball and misses a shot on the six. He puts the cue down carefully, an archbishop surrendering the symbols of the church. He offers a few words of advice on her first shot. She picks up the cue as if it were the Olympic torch and starts off around the table. She puts away the nine, fifteen and the eleven. Bam. Bam. Bam. And this is for you. Pow! The ten. He sits at the bar, bored. He's been playing for so many years. She thinks the game has possibilities, just needs a little work, a little fixing up. She misses a shot on the twelve. He gets up slowly. She is trying to lug a large cement statue of St. Francis into the backyard by herself. He goes to help. Secretly though, it makes him mad. He'll have to fight through the Pacific from island to island again. He's such an old soldier. He picks up his weapon and goes after the deuce and the trey.

IN A TAVERN

It's no use," he says, "she's left me." This is after several drinks. It's as if he had said, "Van Gogh is my favorite painter." It's a cheap print he has added to his collection. He's been waiting all evening to show it to me. He doesn't see it. To him it's an incredible landscape, empty, a desert. "My life is empty." He likes the simplicity. "My life is empty. She won't come back." It is a landmark, like the blue mountains in the distance that never change. The crust of sand gives way with each step, tiny lizards skitter out of the way ... Even after walking all day there is no change in the horizon. "We're lost," he says. "No," I say, "let's go on." He says, "You go on. Take my canteen. You've got a reason to live." "No," I say, "we're in this together and we'll both make it out of here."

THE DUTCH SHOE

She was out of the water for years, since the early fifties maybe, over at the shipyard in Superior. You could see her from the highway, her masts down, sails stowed away. I loved that boat. All the time I was growing up I made plans to buy her someday. What shall I say happened? That my father bought her and put her in the back yard and kept garden tools in the hold? Or that my mother bought her and kept her in the china closet with the jade Buddha and the eight-day clock? That her brass gleams in the firelight, still dry and harmless? No. I bought the Dutch Shoe and sailed to Rangoon and Singapore and a hundred other places. I faced incredible dangers and hardships. I talk loud and drink all night. When I snore I wake bears in the forest and fish in the sea. Early mist rises from the water. Ice forms on the masts. My hair has turned white and my teeth have fallen out. I can't see a thing and I am sailing away.

WALKING THROUGH A WALL

Unlike flying or astral projection, walking through walls is a totally earth-related craft, but a lot more interesting than pot making or driftwood lamps. I got started at a picnic up in Bowstring in the northern part of the state. A fellow walked through a brick wall right there in the park. I said, "Say, I want to try that." Stone walls are best, then brick and wood. Wooden walls with fiberglass insulation and steel doors aren't so good. They won't hurt you. If your wall walking is done properly, both you and the wall are left intact. It is just that they aren't pleasant somehow. The worst things are wire fences. Maybe it's the molecular structure of the alloy or just the amount of give in a fence, I don't know, but I've torn my jacket and lost my hat in a lot of fences. The best approach to a wall is, first, two hands placed flat against the surface; it's a matter of concentration and just the right pressure. You will feel the dry, cool inner wall with your fingers, then there is a moment of total darkness before you step through on the other side.

INVISIBLE

There are moments when a person cannot be seen by the human eye. I'm sure you've noticed this. You might be walking down the street or sitting in a chair when someone you know very well, your mother or your best friend, walks past without seeing you. Later they'll say, "Oh, I must have been preoccupied." Not so. At times we are caught in a warp of space or time and, for a moment, vanish. This phenomenon occurs often among children and old people. No one understands exactly how this happens but some people remain invisible for long periods of time. Most of these do so by choice. They have learned to ride the moment, as a surfer rides the long curl of a wave. How exhilarating it is to ride like that, a feeling of triumph to move from room to room unseen, only the slightest breeze from your passing.

CONFESSIONAL POEM

I have this large tattoo on my chest. It is like a dream I have while I am awake. I see it in the mirror as I shave and brush my teeth, or when I change my shirt or make love. What can I do? I can't remember where I got the tattoo. When in the past did I live such a life? And the price of having such a large tattoo removed must be completely beyond reason. Still, the workmanship of the drawing is excellent, a landscape 8x10 inches in full color, showing cattle going downhill into a small western town. A young man, who might have been my great-grandfather, dressed as a cowboy and holding a rifle, stands at the top of the hill and points down toward the town. The caption beneath the picture reads: "Gosh, I didn't know we were this far west."

The Water's Easy Reach

1985

RESTAURANT OVERLOOKING
LAKE SUPERIOR

Late afternoon. Only a few old men at the bar, drinking and talking quietly. Waitresses for the evening shift begin to arrive. One stands for a moment at the far end of the dining room and looks out the window facing the lake. Snow is falling. The lake is completely obscured, still customers will ask for tables near the window. A few early diners begin to arrive, then others. Soon the room is filled with sounds—people talking, the rattle of dishes, the waitresses hurrying about. The lake is a great silence beneath all the noise. In their hurry the waitresses don't look out the window. Yet they are in her service, silent a moment as they fill the glasses with water.

TAMARACKS

In the evening I am drawn to the tamaracks that bend and straighten in the wind like oarsmen pulling the long boat. It is only the longing to be safely dead, the desire for peace. But perhaps, even in death you would be restless, driving the back roads, a pocket full of change for the telephone, calling across the country at a terrible hour. I think that ghosts are the insomniacs among the dead. The only dead man I ever talked to told me that there used to be a tennis court where my house is now. "That's right. I used to walk here in the evenings when I was a young man." I was impatient. I said, "I want to hear what things are like for you now." He said, "Oh, people always ask me that. Can you explain to a child what it's like to be grown up? It's the same thing. I can tell you this though: times change. I was a blacksmith but I had to get into small engine repair in order to stay in business." "Oh, crap!" I said, and he vanished. The tamaracks accept the darkness just as the little pools of water accept the last portion of light. The air takes the water, leaving the road clear and dry.

PALISADE HEAD

Two hundred feet straight down from here the water boils up on the shore, and farther out is translucent blue-green, rising in even swells. Twenty feet beneath the surface just the tops of big ugly boulders become visible, old men and women at the bottom of stairs whispering and grumbling forever. They save things. They tell drowned sailor jokes. They spend all their lives down there with algae that need water and sunlight, nothing more. I don't know what we are in our most secret selves, but I don't believe it is the free animal we long to be, beautiful and cruel. It is something more simple and more incomprehensible. Looking over the edge makes me a little sick. On those darkest nights of rain and the northeast wind, small stones slip away and are never missed. This is a place of lichen and stubborn trees, a place where only lovers should walk.

NOVEMBER

I do not love the woods it occurs to me, the leafless, brushy, November popple and birch trees that stand around, stand around, crowding the peripheral vision, as if each were waiting to take its place in my consciousness and each falling back to become a part of the line that divides gray earth from gray sky, as undistinguished as gray hair.

Over there one shaft of sunlight penetrates the clouds as if it were an indicator: the finger of God pointing out ... something. What is it Lord? More frozen trees? What is it? It's as if someone leaving on a train says something as the cars begin to move, something through the glass. I can see his lips moving. Gestures. What? I can't hear you. What?

THE LIGHTHOUSE

Light flashes across the water and is gone, like headlights across the wall of a dark room where someone is lying awake. It happens so quickly, no way to take back the things that were said. Your son drove headlong into a train. Your daughter is in a Mexican jail. It's a house passed at eighty miles an hour. Did anyone live there? The night, the sea, the wind and the rocks, the terrible current off shore ... It is good to see the light across the water. It is a warning. This is the place where the land ends and the water begins or the water ends and the land begins. Either way is dangerous.

SAILORS

When the ship gets into port the sailors all go nuts. They get drunk and dance and wake up the next afternoon in the whorehouse. And if a sailor gets thrown in jail he doesn't care because he just got paid and has enough money to get out. None of the sailors wants to go back to the ship. One thing sailors can't stand is the sight of water. One sailor hides out in a laundromat. One makes plans to marry. Another is still drunk. The sailors hate this lousy port. The ship sails at dawn with all hands, but someone has sneaked whiskey aboard. By midnight the crew is drunk and the ship is dead in the water. The captain is furious and shouts over the intercom to the engine room. But they are all asleep, rocked in their little cradle on the sea.

THE HOUSE AT THE LAKE

This house is nearly a hundred years old. Some of the trees around it are even older, tall pines and spruce that shade the many rooms. In this room Great-Grandpa Torgeson spent the last ten years of his life and wouldn't talk to anyone. Grandma knows the story. The kitchen has been remodeled and the bathrooms. The rest of the house is the same as when it was built. Most of the year the house is empty, but everyone vacations here. The family has gotten quite large with Duane and Kathy and their kids and Eileen and her kids and Judy and Art. The children spend the morning wading in the sunny shallows of the lake. Little fish, chubs and shiners, small perch and sunfish nibble at their toes and find food in the sand stirred up from the bottom. Inside the house the talk is usually business, stocks and family property. The children splash and laugh and squeal until someone from the house calls, "Come in children." It's a voice that carries across the deep water of the lake where big muskies with their many rows of teeth glide through whatever grows or was lost down there … *Come in. Time for lunch. Time for sleep.*

COLD

Doors that once opened at a touch refuse to move, and machinery whose friendship you so casually assumed, won't work and is dangerous to touch barehanded. Everything that once seemed so alive is immobile and dumb, but something, long asleep, stirs. A yawn in the beams beneath the floor startles you. What is it? Outside, there is no wind. Smoke from the chimney makes ponderous and eerie shapes that move lightly along the ground by the window, and for a moment before it vanishes in the trees, the shape of someone safely forgotten. "It's no one" you think, to reassure yourself. "No one alive walking around on a night this cold."

FIRST SNOW

By dusk the snow is already partially melted. There are dark patches where the grass shows through, like islands in the sea seen from an airplane. Which one is home? The one I left as a child? They all seem the same now. What became of my parents? What about all those things I started and never finished? What were they? As we get older we become more alone. The man and his wife share this gift. It is their breakfast: coffee and silence, morning sunlight. They make love or they quarrel. They move through the day, she on the black squares, he on the white. At night they sit by fire, he reading his book, she knitting. The fire is agitated. The wind hoots in the chimney like a child blowing in a bottle, happily.

A PHOTOGRAPH

She's been dead fifty years now. This photo was taken in 1902, just a girl, clowning for the camera. But when a baby is born in the family someone says, "See, it has her eyes, her nose." And it's true. The argument continues. "I'm a farmer," I say, "a business man. I can't be wasting time in town, hanging out at the cafe, drinking coffee." It's spring and the roads are impassable. I stand in the barnyard, knee deep in mud, dumbfounded, surrounded by insolent chickens. She says, "I never want to leave here." At night she whispers, "You have never loved me. You think only of yourself. You won't be allowed to enter the Promised Land." Then she giggles and pokes me in the ribs. "The children are asleep now," she says.

SERGEANT NORQUIST

Two years ago I thought seriously about killing myself. I looked at guns in the pawnshops. Then, I don't know why exactly, I turned to God. I have my job at the paper mill and this room, but they mean nothing to me. My real life begins when I put on this uniform and make my rounds. I go to all the bars downtown, even the worst ones along First Street. I say, "Good evening, Salvation Army" and people give me their change, good people mostly. Once in a while a guy will say, "This ain't no church" or something like that, but no one has ever really given me a hard time. Most people respect the uniform. One evening in the Oasis a woman kissed me. I gave her a copy of the *War Cry*. She wasn't an old woman, either, but she had lived hard. I still pray for her. A lot of people talk to me. They tell me their days are hard to get through and I know about that. At night, sometimes, when I can't sleep, I think of all the money I've collected. I close my eyes and see all those nickels and dimes rising from the bars on First Street and from run-down places all over town, from poor people, like a reversed rain, from earth to heaven. I think nothing in heaven would grow if that rain didn't fall.

TWINS

The first baby they brought into my room was a girl. I held her for a few minutes then the nurse took her away. I never saw the baby again or the nurse that brought her. Later another nurse brought the boy, my son. When I told my husband he said it was probably just the effect of the anesthetic, but I made him check. They said there was only one baby born, a boy. I'm certain now there were two. I know the little girl is alive somewhere but I have no idea how to find her. I can only watch her brother for signs ... you know, the way twins sense things about each other. Sometimes I'm afraid when he goes off to school, lost among so many other children. When he comes home in the afternoon I catch him and hold him a moment and look into his eyes before he pulls away to run outside and play with his friends. I can't really say what I'm looking for. I think I'll only know if something is missing, a certain look or a gesture ... I think I'll know if that life dies out in him. I can't explain that to him, of course, or to his father, he would only say I've got too much imagination.

THE WAY

Even if you believe in Jesus there comes a moment when everything sinks. It is that moment when the fire collapses in the grate and the skinny sticks lie there smoldering, broken like the bones of the saints. See, even though you have come only this far your Eveready batteries have begun to fail and it *is* a swamp ... or say it's a city street, but the first person you meet is a small man wearing a straw hat and striped overalls that are clean and starched. His hands and feet are very small and only the tips of his shiny black shoes stick out from the big legs of his pants. He has something in his pocket that shines, a cross or a switchblade. He asks your name and says he knows some of your family. He's crazy. He shows you a dance in which the movements are something like those of a goose. It is called "The Dance of People Who Look Just Alike." He says he will tell you a story about a woman he knows who has lived for years above a grocery store. He knows her very well and will take you to meet her. Now you have lingered here so long it is growing dark. There is no one on the street. You will have to spend the night here and you had hoped to make it at least to Cincinnati.

LIBRARY

I sit down at a table and open a book of poems and move slowly into the shadow of tall trees. They are white pines, I think. The ground is covered with soft brown needles and there are signs that animals have come here silently and vanished before I could catch sight of them. But here the trail edges into a cedar swamp: wet ground, dead fall and rotting leaves. I move carefully but rapidly, pleased with myself. Someone else comes and sits down at the table, a serious looking young man with a large stack of books. He takes a book from the top of the stack and opens it. The book is called *How to Get a High-Paying Job*. He flips through it and lays it down and picks up another and pages through it quickly. It is titled *Moving Ahead*. We are moving ahead more rapidly now, through a second growth of popple and birch, our faces scratched and our clothes torn by the underbrush. We are moving even faster, marking the trail, followed closely by bulldozers and crews from the paper company.

An Almost Human Gesture

1987

A QUIET PLACE

I have come to understand my love for you. I came to you like a man, world-weary, looking for a quiet place. The gas station and grocery store, the church, the abandoned school, a few old houses, the river with its cool shady spots ... Good fishing. How I've longed for a place like this! As soon as I got here I knew I'd found it. Tomorrow the set production and camera crews arrive. We can begin filming on Monday: the story of a man looking for a quiet place.

THE UKRAINIAN EASTER EGG

It is quite different from the ordinary Ukrainian Easter Egg because of the pictures. On one side the sun is setting over Los Angeles and opposite, soldiers sitting in the muddy trenches. They look cold, smoking cigarettes. Here is the violin hidden in the soup kettle and there is a family of cats living in an abandoned gas station. There are so many pictures: the barbed wire and the road through the forest, the ducks, the radio, the yellow, smoky fires along the railroad track where the lovers are taking a walk. In the morning the elders of the village decide what must be done. A brave man must ride the fastest horse and deliver the egg. The journey is long, the roads are dangerous, the egg must be given only to the Czar.

MEDICINE

He sits in a chair and does not move for a long time. He thinks he should do something, take some action, but he doesn't know what. Nothing seems worth the effort. He leans his head back to rest against the wall, stretches out his legs and is still again. The way he sits he seems a part of something else, one side of a mountain perhaps, the way it slopes down to flat land. This year the crops burned up, livestock died. The ground is cracked and dry. The little girl is sick. The wife hardly speaks and lies down each night beside the sick child. The farmer walks out to look at the sky, hands at his sides, followed by a skinny dog. It is nearly dark. The moon rises making a shadowy light on the trail. A man on horseback dressed in black is coming down the trail, the man from the medicine show, bringing his bottles down from the mountain. Bottles of pure water. With each careful step of the pony the bottles in the saddlebags clink together. The man is singing quietly to himself.

WAR SURPLUS

Aisle after aisle of canvas and khaki, helmets and mess kits, duffle bags, pea coats, gas masks ... Somewhere there is a whole field of abandoned aircraft, all kinds, P-38s, B-25s ... All you have to do is wait until dark, climb over the fence, pull the blocks from the wheels, climb in, start the engines and taxi out to the strip. It's easy. You can fly without ever having had a lesson.

A beautiful woman dressed in black sits on a bench near a grave. A tall man in dress uniform stands beside her and puts his hand on her shoulder. She says, "I come here often, it is so peaceful." He says, "Before John died, he asked me to look after you." They embrace. Behind them are many neat rows of white crosses extending over a green hill where the flag is flying proudly.

The engines make a deep drone, a comforting sound, and the light from the instrument panel tells you everything is stable and right. Below are silver-tufted clouds and tiny enemy towns, lovely toy towns, all lighted by the bomber's moon.

THE ICE FISHERMAN

From here he appears as a black spot, one of the shadows that today has found it necessary to assume solid form, and along with the black jut of shoreline far to the left, is the only break in the undifferentiated gray of ice and overcast sky. Here is a man going jiggidy-jig-jig in a black hole. Depth and the current are of only incidental interest to him. He's after something big, something down there that is pure need, something that, had it the wherewithal, would swallow him whole. Right now nothing is happening. The fisherman stands and straightens, back to the wind. He stays out on the ice all day.

MARGARET LUOMA

At her age a fall could have meant a serious injury, a sprained ankle or a broken hip. Luckily there was only a bruise and the terrible embarrassment. She pulled away from the young man who helped her to her feet, said "Thank you, I'm all right" and went on her way as quickly as she could without looking back. But she couldn't forget about it. His face ... like a photograph on the piano, thoughtful, always young. "All that concern," she thought. "What did he care?" It began to seem as though he'd caused the bruises, actually pushed her down. She didn't need him. She was old now. A lifetime of love wasted.

BREAD

Bread rising! The intoxicating smell of yeast. And bread fresh from the oven. Someone loves me and has left warm bread. When bread is broken, the life hidden within presents itself, a thousand little holes, windows open for the first time. In one booth near the window four old women are drinking tea. They are dressed in old-fashioned clothes, layer on layer, suits and furs, jewelry handed down for generations. One woman names the year of her mother's birth, and another the day her husband died: his clothes still hanging in the closet. They talk calmly, quietly, the spring sunlight coming through the glass to touch the backs of their hands.... Sit down. Share this bread. As we talk you can explain the ordinary things. I will play some music for you that isn't mine.

THE HERMIT

It's true that the best part of a trip lies between the starting place and the destination. The fun is in the getting there. And it's not always what you see along the way but what you can't see, or can just barely see: the place where the spruce and hemlock fade into the mist and smoke rises from some hidden cabin. The man, who has lived here twenty-five years, winter and summer, alone, comes out carrying a shotgun when you approach. Not unfriendly, just cautious. But he has nothing to hide. He talks about county taxes. He doesn't keep a dog. Dogs run the deer in the spring when there's a crust on the snow. It doesn't take a big dog to bring down a deer, either. He says he's shot maybe thirty, thirty-five dogs since he's lived here. As he talks mosquitoes land on his face and neck but he doesn't bother to brush them away. Maybe he doesn't regret not wasting his youth in unrequited love. Probably he never thinks of it. Or if he does, only absently, the way you notice cars passing on the interstate a mile from here.

APPLEJACK

Wilma worked sixteen years for a plumbing and heating company and never married. She lived with her mother in a little house out in Arnold Township. And her mother, who was crazy from drinking applejack, would hide behind the door when Wilma came home from work and try to stab her with a butcher knife. Wilma didn't know what to do. When she thought of having her put in a rest home, the old lady would cry and Wilma's aunt in Seattle would write letters saying, "Don't you dare put my sister in a rest home." This went on for years and Wilma began drinking applejack too. When the old woman finally died, Wilma quit her job, lived alone in the house and wore her mother's clothes.

I know of a man killed driving his pickup a hundred miles an hour, and another who left his wife and family and ran off with a red-headed high school girl. They had been drinking applejack.

Now, when the birch and maple leaves have fallen and blow nervously around the roads, the juice from this year's apples has begun to ferment. This is no ordinary applejack. The bottles may remain hidden for years, deep down among the roots and the dead, before someone takes the first sip.

MARLENE NOLUND

She's packed the kids off to spend the weekend with their father. At last she has the place to herself, a rented farmhouse, a couple dozen chickens, a pickup that works part-time and a child support check she finally managed to get from her ex-husband. His problem was that he didn't want anything much. He was happy being a bricklayer or being in the army, happy just hanging around the house. She puts on her best dress and stands in front of the mirror brushing her hair. She looks good, a little big in the chest maybe, but good for being the mother of two. It's mid-afternoon and the whole weekend is ahead. The summer wind nags at the house and flaps the blind at the window behind her so that it sounds like someone impatiently turning the pages of a newspaper. She imagines a man there, lying on the bed, glancing up occasionally to hurry her along, jingling the change in his pocket. It makes her nervous and angry. She fidgets with the dress, extracts a pair of earrings from the clutter of perfume and baby bottles on the bureau, smears her makeup. She hurries. It isn't what she wants.

A NEW CAR

He comes in late Saturday night, drunk. She pretends to be asleep when he comes to bed. Long before he wakes, Sunday morning, she is up and dressed. She dresses the child and drives away into the early fog. She drives 80 mph over the blacktop country roads for several hours. When he wakes the sun is shining and the house is quiet. He has a hangover and thinks perhaps he has been robbed. He feels his pants pocket for his wallet. He stands at the window and looks out at the empty driveway. When she returns he is sitting at the kitchen table drinking coffee. "Where have you been?" he says. She says, "I had to take the baby to Sunday school, I can't depend on you to do it." He returns to the window and looks at the car. It's getting worn out he thinks, needs brakes and tires. He wishes he could afford a new one.

THE BLIND MAN

He comes down the hill at a slight angle to the sidewalk, hesitantly, moving his red-tipped white cane from side to side until it touches the fender of a lavender Pontiac parked at the curb. Then he stops. He reaches out with his left hand until he touches the cold metal pole of a No Parking sign, pulls himself close, stands with his arm wrapped around the pole in the narrow space between pole and car, waits and listens. He seems unsure, seems to have difficulty sorting the various sounds. Traffic to the right, traffic behind, wind blowing uphill from the lake, the sound of a few leaves on the concrete. No passersby. End of the day, end of fall. He listens, head slightly raised, hat pushed back, eyes closed. He is neither young nor old: a man between a car and a pole. He waits a long time. Then he moves his cane to the right, up into the rear wheelwell of the car, then away to the left. He releases the pole and takes two careful steps downhill, moving the cane in front of him.

PAAVO WIRKKILA

There is something about a clearing that makes me feel uneasy, something too sunny and optimistic about this break in the constant shade, those nervous poplars and gloomy spruce all turned to face an open space as if they expected something to happen here: the blank page on which something must be written.

Paavo Wirkkila got an idea, cleared the land and grew hay. Nothing else grows very well around here. He kept a horse to help with the hay then fed the hay to the horse. A limited plan. When the old man died he left the buildings to fall, left the clearing to the county and sapling popple trees. He also left this heap of stones he'd cleared from the field, not a monument, no part of his plan, just an annoyance he tried to push out of his earthly way.

APPOINTED ROUNDS

At first he refused to deliver junk mail because it was stupid, all those deodorant ads, moneymaking ideas and contests. Then he began to doubt the importance of the other mail he carried. He began to randomly select first class mail for non-delivery. After he had finished his mail route each day he would return home with his handful of letters and put them in the attic. He didn't open them and never even looked at them again. It was as if he were an agent of Fate, capricious and blind. In the several years before he was caught, friends vanished, marriages failed, business deals fell through. Toward the end he became more and more bold, deleting houses, then whole blocks from his route. He began to feel he'd been born in the wrong era. If only he could have been a Pony Express rider galloping into some prairie town with an empty bag, or the runner from Marathon collapsing in the streets of Athens, gasping, "No news."

FROST FLOWERS

In the morning people go off to work all wrapped and bundled, through frozen doors, over cracking snow, huffing and puffing, each fueled by some simmering private indignation: low pay, something that was said at break ... The sun is far away on the southern horizon, a vague hope, more distant than the Caribbean. Eight below zero at eleven o'clock. The coffee boils and grows bitter. All afternoon, the same old thing, knucklebone of mastodon, stews on the stove. The radiator hisses at the long shadows that finally engulf the winter day. Lights come on for a time in the houses and go out one by one. We breathe deeply of the dark, we exhale great plumes and fronds that form on the windows, intricate icy blossoms open around us all night.

32 DEGREES F.

The thermometer says exactly 32 degrees, freezing or melting. Neither here nor there ... at the border, in a room without enough chairs, waiting with your bundle of possessions and the uneasy feeling that none of these things will be adequate on the other side. Outside the window a single drop of water hangs on the tip of an icicle for hours. A long time ago she showed me how to take the blossom at the base, snap off the stem, then carefully withdraw the pistil, pulling it slowly down until the little globe of nectar poised there, ready to take on the tongue. The single drop distilled from a lifetime falls to shatter on the frozen ground and the mindless soul flies away to its heaven on the honeysuckle south wind that's come five hundred miles over the snow.

THE FLOOD

Every so often, a girl calls me on the phone and tells me that she loves me, can't live without me, etc. The first time she called I was intrigued and flattered, naturally. But when I asked her name she ignored me and went right on talking. "Could we meet somewhere?" Again she ignored the question. Finally I became irritated and hung up. Obviously it was some kind of joke. She called several more times over the next few months and each time the result was the same. "What's the point?" I ask. "I love you," she says. A few weeks ago the bridge on 21st Street washed out. People came from all over town to help with the work and to watch the river overflow its banks and pour through the streets, the first flood in many years. Men were hard at work piling up sandbags to hold back the water. Near where I was standing, a pay telephone kept ringing and ringing. Finally, since no one else did, I answered. I thought perhaps it was someone calling with instructions for the flood control workers, but no. It was a man having trouble with his refrigerator. I guess he thought I was a repairman. No sooner had he hung up than the phone rang again: a woman looking for her child. No, I hadn't seen him. Call after call came in. It was as if people were actually telephoning the flood. For some reason I kept answering the phone. Then she called. "Hello," a pause. "Hello," I said again. "Louis," she said, "Louis—is that you?" I hung up the phone and stepped out of the booth. It was a relief to be in the open air again. I stood a moment looking at the muddy water while the phone continued to ring.

All Tangled Up
with the Living

1991

THE LOST BOY

When Jason did not come home from school on the bus Barbara began to worry. She went next door to ask if Bobby, who rode the same bus, had seen Jason. Bobby remembered seeing Jason but didn't think he got on the bus. Bobby's mother, Teresa, said, "Oh, he probably just decided to walk." Teresa thought Barbara was a silly woman who fussed over her children. Bobby and Chris set out to look for Jason. It was an adventure, a search through the Dark Continent. Barbara used Teresa's phone to call the school. Meanwhile, Jason returned home, went in the back door and up to his room. Through the open window he could hear his mother in the next yard. He flopped down on the bed and looked at comics. He could hear his mother talking about calling the police. He lay looking at the big crack in the ceiling. He thought about what it was like to be lost. He thought he could hear voices, far away, calling his name.

OUT-OF-THE-BODY TRAVEL

Body and soul are linked as in a marriage, a sort of three-legged race team, and are usually comfortable with this arrangement. If the soul is forced to travel alone it does not wing its way over wide water, does not fly skimming the treetops. No, the soul shuffles along like any body, eating at lunch counters, listening to conversation in the bus station restroom ... "Fifty cents? I think I can get fifty cents ...," riding the bus all through the dark night, watching the distant, singular lights go past, wondering all the while if this trip was really necessary. Meanwhile the body sits, inert, staring at the T.V., needing a shave, a nail trim.

A PORTRAIT OF THE MASTER

In this picture Jesus stands, as if addressing his followers, with his right arm partially raised, his index finger, slightly crooked, pointing upward. His left arm extends downward, palm open. He looks as he often does in pictures, white robe, sandals, beard neatly trimmed. His hair is rather long but clean. His face is calm, unwearied, because Jesus maintains, even thrives under the pressure of constant travel and the demands of those who flock to him. These are a ragged bunch, malcontents, the disenfranchised, those for whom heaven is impossible, the only ones who show any interest at all in what he has to say. They want help; they come to tell their stories, to ask questions, but mainly to listen. They have the sense that He is one of them, only better. And though the word He brings is difficult, it is the saying that is important. We must continually explain ourselves to ourselves. There is no one else to listen. He says again: "Here is the earth. Here is the sky."

DOWN TO THE RIVER

When Daddy married Mama
she made him go down
to the river and get baptized.
When Daddy went down
the congregation sang
We shall all come together at the river.
When the preacher pushed him under,
when the water rolled over his head,
Grandma said she saw the devil
rise up from the water
and shake himself all over like a dog,
then wade to the other shore.
Grandma didn't say where he went from there.
Grandma said for sure
we will all rise again.

In the yellow light of the room
you brush out your hair
a hundred long smooth strokes
and I lie still on the bed.
What can we do? I ask.
There is no answer.
When the light is turned out
it is so dark I can't see
my hand in front of my face
but it is you I reach out to
in these hard times
no other.

Rise up! Rejoice!
Rise up in the rainy night

like a mushroom from the damp forest floor,
a destroying angel
clothed in robes of purest white,
a simple and deadly life.
Let each day be a day of praise and thanksgiving.
If you are lost in the forest
eat the mushrooms and die.

This is the river Jordan,
the healing stream,
troublesome waters,
the high wind of the stratosphere
in which the ragged earth is bathed.
I hold out my hands.
These are lands to the left and right,
little islands called the Lucid Moments
completely covered by the high tide.
I wiggle my fingers.
These are fishes that swim in the sea.
Any moment now you will go under
so there's no reason to be afraid.
If someone grabs your left hand
or your right hand
and asks if you want to be saved
tell him no.

OKLAHOMA

On this rolling and open prairie anything higher than a horse's head is obtrusive and out of place. Grain elevators and oil wells strung together by right-angled roads, seems altogether the wrong approach. Go south two miles, take a right ... A tornado doesn't bother. It blows cross-country rearranging the debris to suit itself. Anything built here should, like open shelving, allow the wind to pass right through. Suppose the books fall, someone will pick them up, dust them off and replace them. Shakespeare, the Bible, there was something there, just beyond us, by the cottonwood and the dry creekbed, that shivered slightly in the afternoon heat as it moved toward the house, that might yet pass, praise God, taking only a leaf or a shingle. I still have a few friends scattered across the state. When we say hello there's a distance in our eyes as if we had found ourselves in a field two miles from home.

ADAM

At first it was okay naming the beasts of the field and the fowls of the air ... dog, cat, cow ... but it was a time consuming job and after awhile it became boring ... slender loris, bridled guillemot ... And the insects drove him crazy. Then there were the plants and rocks. Sunrise to sunset, the same thing. He didn't want to just name the things Jehovah had made. He wanted to recombine the elements to make something significant, a creation of his own. He just needed some time off to think, to plan. He wanted a convertible, something sporty, so he could take Eve for a little drive, lovely Eve dressed in her snakeskin miniskirt with the matching bag.

AMATEUR ARTIST

He sees that the eyes are wrong. The left eyelid should curve more. He erases and draws the line again. He has no ease with this, no grace, no freedom. It's like work. He wants to get it right. He looks at her photo again and then at the drawing. The drawing looks wrong, too stiff, and unnatural. He leaves the eyes and goes to the breasts. He likes this better, the easy graceful sweep of the pencil. Now he sees that the mouth is not right. The paper is nearly worn through in places from erasing and redrawing. How easily everything can go wrong. A misplaced mark becomes a deformity. Another mark, and the mood is completely changed. She looks out at him with eyes slightly askew and it's apparent that she is not pleased. Whoever this is.

NO MATTER HOW FAR YOU DRIVE

I sat between Mamma and Daddy.
My sister sat on Mamma's lap.
Daddy drove. Fields, telephone poles ...
I watched the sun go down.
"Never look straight at the sun,
it could ruin your eyes."
No matter how far you drive
you can't get to the sun.
I touched the pearly knob
of the gearshift lever
and felt the vibration in my fingers.
It made Daddy nervous.
"Never mess around with that.
You could ruin the car,
cause an accident."
It was dark, the sun gone to China.
Out there in the dark,
fourteen lights. I counted. Fourteen.
Rabbits ran in front of the car
from one black ditch to the other.
I didn't know where we were.
I could see the red light on the dashboard
and the light of Daddy's Lucky Strike
that broke into a million sparks behind us
when he threw it out the window.

BLACK SPRUCE

Most of us live out our lives
on the edge of something:
bankruptcy, greatness, sanity ...
If you could stand back far enough
it might be possible to imagine the forest.
Up close it's trees:
jack pine, balsam, spruce,
alder and popple.
Here the dead remain visible,
all tangled up with the living.
Nothing is simplified
by this bucolic setting
but complication becomes more palpable
and confusion is manifest
as silence.

In the city it seems no one
treats you as a human being.
The woods, on the other hand,
are full of things that do,
that run if you come too close.

It's lonely.
Who will you talk to?
Who will you invite to your birthday party?
Bears overindulge and fall asleep.
Owls can never remember anyone's name.

If you look a ways down the road
there is a light,
a kind of bluish light,
illuminating a pile of used tires

outside a closed up gas station.
All around you the black spruce trees
are full of instruction,
pointing this way and that,
waving hello, goodbye.
Here's the road to Brimson, to Wawina.
This way ... no, here.
Here is the swamp, the riverbed,
the glacial esker.
Drive right in.
There's warm porcupine on the blacktop,
cold water in the ditch.
Truly a table is prepared in the wilderness.
When you have walked far enough
you will sit down.

THE MARGINS

Out here between nowhere
and the highway, halfway
to town, in the scrap woods,
where the taxes don't kill you,
are places scraped out of
the popple trees—a well,
septic tank, a mobile home,
broken cars and snowmobiles.
Out here energy
has been transformed into
unstable mass. Alcohol,
divorce, mechanical failure....
We live from paycheck to
paycheck, lunging after each
as if climbing a ladder
too large for us, long
abandoned by the angels,
reaching only the high
uncluttered sadness of old age.

AUTOMOBILE REPAIR

It's raining and the car stalls with Mama, the kids and a full load of laundry inside. At least the warning lights still work. You raise the hood and find yourself staring, once again, into the void. Fuel pump? Alternator? The trick is to keep this thing running without spending any money, akin to making something from nothing. Thus Jehovah, confronted with a similar difficulty, simply began assembling the salvaged parts of the previous universe. Once you have located the problem you're ready (two or three cups of coffee will help) to plunge into the mud and grease. This time it's easy. The wire from the coil to the distributor has fallen off. It's running again—bald tires, broken exhaust, rust ...

ALL-NIGHT CHINESE CAFE

Ivor Knutson and his best friend, who was half Indian so everyone called him Chief, were in Ole's Tavern one night arguing which are better, dogs or cats. Both were drunk and when Chief threatened him with a knife, Ivor ran out of the tavern. Half an hour later he was back, firing away with a .22 pistol. He managed not only to kill Chief but Ole, the owner, as well, and to wound three other people before the police arrived. Ivor himself was killed two years later in a prison fight. Those times are referred to now as "the good old days in Ole's Tavern." After the bars closed at night nobody wanted to go home so we went to the all-night Chinese cafe where it was warm and food was cheap. I remember there were bottles of orange soda in the window as a display. The liquid in the bottles had faded over the years so that it was almost clear.

IN THE STREETS

He carries everything he owns in a paper bag. What are you? A broken alarm clock? A returnable pop bottle? Once, on this very corner, a man hit him in the mouth. That's why some of his teeth are missing. It was drink made that man hit him. He never drinks. He waits for you every day with his hand out. Every day without fail. It's a wonder he's still alive. The coldest days he spends at the public library. But where does he go at night? The moon is shining now at four in the afternoon and down here it's all wind and shadows. In the streets with the blowing snow and newspapers he carries on the same argument with his parents, though they have been dead thirty years. At the mouths of alleys he pauses ... He is an only child. All he wants is his share.

GREEN TOMATO

This morning
after the first frost,
there is a green tomato
among the Kleenex,
combs and loose change,
the more usual clutter
on the dresser.
That's the way it is
around here—
things picked up,
put down, lost
or forgotten. Here is the possibility
of next year's crop,
even more,
in one green tomato.
It makes me smile
to see it there,
newly discovered,
confident and
mysterious as the face
of my young son
who comes to the bedroom
early, ready to play.
There is no point in
my telling you too much
of what makes me
happy or sad.
I did not wake to find,
at this moment,
in this unlikely place,
only my own life.

SOUP

In the yard of her place on a branch of the Knife,
she mixed in the big cast iron pot,
aspen bark, birch root, garlic and beets,
spruce gum, willow twigs, water from the creek,
(tasting slightly of crankcase oil)
road kill, fish heads, cinnamon and leeks.
She added onion and bitter herbs
a touch of sumac, pepper and salt,
withered apples, cabbage and gnarled potatoes.
All day the smoke swirled through bare branches
and the crows overhead circled and dived.
When she took a taste from the big wooden spoon
it wasn't right.

Each ingredient should blend so that each taste
was a reminiscence, sensibly tempered, a joy,
a tonic against the ague and the grippe,
against old age and the grinding cold winter.
It wasn't right this year, flat somehow…
It needed something. But what was it?
Anytime now the guests might arrive.

THE PAINTER

After he has covered the earth the painter is ready to start on the sky. Beauty requires constant attention and, anyway, it's a living. What color is the sky today? Blue. He stirs the paint, pours half into his bucket and starts up the ladder one step at a time, slowly. He climbs above the trees, above the cows grazing in the field, above the rivers and mountains. He leans to one side and spits—a long way down. He doesn't like it much. He hooks his bucket to the ladder and dips his brush. He makes the first even stroke.

THE OTHER PEOPLE

One sees them, then forgets. They appear as if in the peripheral vision. They may be what the Irish call "the little people" but they are not really little, a bit smaller perhaps, like large children ... I'm not sure. They must inhabit the forest, the night. They sometimes appear in the blue-green light that precedes a thunderstorm. Once I think there were many, but as we humans more and more take over the other places of the world their numbers diminish ... I think. One is never sure. They appear and the contact brings forgetting, whole blocks of the past vanish from memory. Perhaps this is true for them also, for sometimes they appear startled, unsure. Perhaps nowadays they inhabit basements, warehouses, lockers, scrap woods, the marginal land outside of town. I don't know. They are like us but not exactly. Occasionally one will stand beside you as you wait in line. One of them is busy removing the labels from canned goods in the grocery. Hey! Then you have forgotten, lost the thread of a long, involved argument.

FISH OUT OF WATER

When he finally landed the fish it seemed so strange, so unlike other fishes he'd caught, so much bigger, more silvery, more important, that he half expected it to talk, to grant his wishes if he returned it to the water. But the fish said nothing, made no pleas, gave no promises. His fishing partner said, "Nice fish, you ought to have it mounted." Other people who saw it said the same thing, "Nice fish ... ;" So he took it to the taxidermy shop but when it came back it didn't look quite the same. Still, it was an impressive trophy. Mounted on a big board the way it was, it was too big to fit in the car. In those days he could fit everything he owned into the back of his Volkswagen but the fish changed all that. After he married, a year or so later, nothing would fit in the car. He got a bigger car. Then a new job, children ... The fish moved with them from house to house, state to state. All that moving around took its toll on the fish, it began to look worn, a fin was broken off. It went into the attic of the new house. Just before the divorce became final, when he was moving to an apartment, his wife said, "Take your goddamn fish." He hung the fish on the wall before he'd unpacked anything else. The fish seemed huge, too big for this little apartment. Boy, it was big. He couldn't imagine he'd ever caught a fish that big.

NORTHERN RIVER

for Phil and Connie

Our map must have been drawn
by an amateur cartographer who,
too anxious to please his readers,
provided imaginary portages
around real rapids.
Muskeg, brush, blackflies and mosquitoes ...;
In one place we had to crash through
a stickery spruce thicket
so dense it must have taken two hours
to go not quite a quarter mile,
to find the river again below the falls.
At a stone-circled backwater
topped with foam and beaver stick flotsam,
we put in finally—weary, scratched up—
slipped out into midstream
and let the water carry the canoe.

We paddle and the canoe moves along
a little faster than the water moves,
and the trees along the shore go past
a little faster than the trees on the hill.
Our rhythmic motion delights us bow and stern.
We say, "It couldn't be better than this!"
"This is perfect, and as long as we follow the river
it's impossible to ever get lost. Right?"

At times the river runs full of intent
between its banks of granite and gabbro
where the tall pines dig into the cracks,
then it falls, turns back on itself and slows
to wander around for hours in the swamp,

muttering the word or two
it has always known.
All that experience good for nothing, finally.
No one remembers the ice age
or much of what happened last week.
One gives up eating raw onions,
and the amorous pursuit of young women
gives way to the cultivation of hair in the ears.
Here on either side—
one-eyed, half-realized—
birch stump, moss and rock,
those shapes that appeared sometimes at night
in your childhood room
and since have waited for your return.
Always lift your hat as you pass
and say, "How do?"

We've wedged ourselves in for the night
among some spruce and balsam
that don't welcome us.
From a nearby blasted white pine
a raven repeats his warning:
"I am a raven. Please do not
violate my personal space."
We grope around in the dark at our feet
for sticks to feed the fire
until fuel and brandy are exhausted
and we've begun our sideways drift to sleep.
The river continues all night
fumbling towards Hudson Bay
in an evolution that goes beyond our participation.
We aren't going that far.
A child said: "A long time ago
people used to be monkeys,
but not you and me."

CLEAR CUT

Short stuff, crew cut,
jack pine and popple,
pulpwood for paper mills;
newspapers and books of poems,
not worth the paper they're printed on.
Something comes up to the tent
but when you look there's nothing.
Silence, the wilderness.
It's annoying.
In this light you can see everything
as a series of lines, planes and angles:
the division of property.
You take the phonograph,
I'll take the records.
You take the car,
I'll take the bus.
You take the baby,
I'll take the bathwater.
It's completely practical;
behavior modification.
If your eye offends you,
pluck it out.

THE TENT

Concave on the windward side, convex on the lee, it
snaps and strains the ropes. Green nylon not quite the
color of the forest, it is the flag of nothing in particular,
a banner that proclaims we will not be here very long, a
modest shelter shedding only the lightest rains. Like home
anywhere, pitched on an unsheltered point, the tent wants
to fly into the air, heave sideways into the lake.

EVENING

At dusk the light
chooses carefully
the things it loves;
the water, the white
belly of the fish
the hands of the fisherman,
the bright blade of the knife.

RETURN PORTAGE

First the canoe,
400 rods over a hilly trail
then back for the packs
and the fishing poles
and one last look at the lake.

I wish it would always be like this.
Move up, go back,
pick everything up,
leave nothing
but the pines,
the lake,
the fall afternoon.

PINE SISKINS

All aggression and appetite they fight for space at the feeder, ruffling and flapping. Such rudeness from so delicate a bird. The weight ratio of brain to body enhances their capacity for flight but limits their talent for reflection and conjecture. They live out their daily lives in instinctual confusion, dropping several seeds for every one they eat. It's a folly that serves a need, feeding a squirrel, rabbit or mouse. One male sidesteps toward a female and she sidesteps away but not very far. Some unseen signal, some slight movement or sound, sends the entire flock into the air; each bird held perfectly aloft, unencumbered by engines of faith.

MR. WATKINS

When Mr. Watkins discovered one of the old gods dead in the crawl space under the house he put on his overalls, tied a bandana over his nose and mouth and worked his way beneath the low cobweb-covered floor joists on his belly. He planned to drag it out by the heels but as soon as he touched the corpse there was a flash and a pop like a downed powerline. Mr. Watkins' heart stopped and the air smelled of ozone. The resulting fire completely destroyed the house and the garage.

Stray dogs, squirrels, flights of harpies roosting on the TV antenna, angels and devils only too ready to spirit you away ...

At night Mr. Watkins used to patrol his 75 by 150 foot lot with a flashlight. You could hear his cough; see the light bobbing over the damp grass in summer, over the snowbanks in winter. Mr. Watkins was an old man and forgot things easily but he knew where the property lines were drawn and, by god, if you don't know that you don't know anything.

VIBRATION

The windowpane vibrates at a constant, barely audible frequency. One doesn't notice it at first, but it can be quite annoying once you become aware of it. The water in this glass vibrates when I set it on the table—waves in a miniature ocean. The glass vibrates; therefore the table is moving. Put your fingers here or there and you can feel it. And the floor. Perhaps there is some large machine nearby working day and night, some tremendous project that never gets completed. If you look long enough at anything—the house next door, the leafless ash tree, the old woman in the ratty fur walking her overweight dog—you can see the slight blurring, a kind of blue-white outline, an uncertainty, a sadness as each thing separates itself from the air.

THE WRISTWATCH

In the morning, after I dressed, I looked for my wristwatch on the nightstand and discovered that it was missing. I looked in the drawer and on the floor, under the bed. It was nowhere to be seen. I looked in the bathroom, checked the pockets of my jacket, my pants. I looked downstairs in the kitchen, the living room. I went out to check the car. I went to the basement and looked through the laundry. I went back upstairs and looked everywhere again. I said, "Have you seen my watch?" to my wife, my children. "I'm sure I left it on the nightstand." I became obsessed with finding the watch. I removed all the drawers from the dresser one by one, emptying their contents onto the bedroom floor. Impossible. Someone must have come in the night and taken it. A watch thief, who with great stealth and cunning, disdaining silverware, jewelry, cameras, fine art, money, had made his way to the bedside and stolen my Timex wristwatch. Perhaps my wife has, for years, been harboring some secret grudge and finally, unable to bear it any longer, took revenge by flushing my watch down the toilet. Maybe my seven-year-old is supporting a drug habit. One thing is certain: nothing, nothing was the way I thought it was.

CLOUD ATLAS

—Eh! qu'aimes-tu donc, extraordinaire étranger?
—J'aime les nuages…les nuages qui passent…
là-bas… là-bas…les merveilleux nuages!

– Baudelaire

I. Cumulus

One lives in the world
more quietly, sometimes, than one would like.
And yes, beyond this world is another.
One lives with that world too,
as with a crazy uncle
who comes downstairs occasionally
for whiskey and cigarettes,
then it's back up to his room
where he's working on a plan
of significance to the world at large,
thinking …
It's quiet.
He's right though,
beyond this second world is yet another.
World piles on world in a compact and towering mass
that, with its domes and canyons,
resembles a cauliflower
or the human brain.

Each moment, though it passes silently,
is a turmoil of emotions,
our smallest actions driven by workings
more complex than those of a watch
but less precise.

(I lean toward you over the piña coladas
as our conversation drifts from
the international monetary crisis
to your favorite music.)
We expect certain grace with all this energy
the way the Arethusa, under Liberian registry,
slides across the oily water to her berth
easily, swiftly ...
a little too swiftly perhaps ... Full astern!
White water boils up behind,
seagulls fly away ...
Too late.
There will be an investigation,
the captain relieved of his command.

We give names to the winds aloft
and expect them to arrange everything.
Because of Love a man will leave his home
and spend the rest of his life in Pittsburgh.
It's frightening.
One thing leads to another.

II. Stratus

Everywhere you look are the poor, the old and sick,
those who must count the cost of everything,
each tooth, each hair numbered,
each icy step a risk,
those for whom one and one and one
add up to nothing, no horizon,
a shuffling walk from bed
to window where the muted light
plays on the building next door.

Today air and water have fused,
no lake, no sky, no horizon ...
an apartment wall.
A Kline poster, books, cinder blocks and boards,
teapot, frying pan, coffee cups ...
the dishes pile up in the sink.
The faucet drips, drips
as grey afternoon ticks into evening.
A woman moves in perhaps
bringing curtains, a rug,
a couple of geckos.
But you, preoccupied,
listen to the careful tick, tick
considering the possible combinations,
waiting for the tumblers to fall.

The colors are black and white
or combinations thereof.
The answers are yes and no,
yes no yes no no no and yes
or maybe
when seen from a distance.
From here it is possible
to think in the grandest terms
yet someone walking just behind you
has disappeared
between one and zero.

III. Cirrus

It seems to me you enjoyed
shattering the fine bone china
though the focus of our discussion

escapes me. Perhaps there was
a wisp of hair that curled
in front of your ear that you
brushed back as you spoke.
I've forgotten because I kissed you,
probably, and took your hand awhile.
Beneath that translucent skin
the tiny veins branch
to invisible capillaries:
the ancient delta culture bred
to a fine nervous instability.
Perhaps so much detail
left us confused, confounded
by a superfluity of information:
shoe sizes, opinions about Nietzsche. . .

One wearies of matters of substance.
I recommend those moments
that, without reason, last a lifetime:
the girl on the shore
brushing her teeth as we sailed away,
a glimpse of a face, a shoulder
in a doorway;
moments like music,
truth untroubled by meaning.
Of course, there's not,
at this altitude, enough oxygen
for a swallow, let alone
a family of four.

That first glimpse, as the plane turned,
of the Sangre de Cristos
with their lacework of snow
set against the western sky,

patterns repeated in cloud, in sand,
in sun on water all seemed, somehow,
like mileposts on the true way,
indicators of something that
would finally reveal itself.
Yet, at any moment the wind
could peel back the pie-crust aluminum
exposing the sham, the skein of wire,
the ridiculous construct of kitchenware
and string that could not,
under any circumstance, allow for flight...

Still, we seem to be moving right along.

UNFORTUNATE LOCATION

In the front yard there are three big white pines, older than anything in the neighborhood except the stones. Magnificent trees that toss their heads in the wind like the spirited black horses of a troika. It's hard to know what to do, tall dark trees on the south side of the house, an unfortunate location, blocking the winter sun. Dark and damp. Moss grows on the roof, the porch timbers rot and surely the roots have reached the old bluestone foundation. At night, in the wind, a tree could stumble and fall, killing us in our beds. The needles fall year after year making an acid soil where no grass grows. We rake the fallen debris, nothing to be done, we stand around with sticks in our hands. Wonderful trees.

GHOSTS

Everything about them is vague. They drift about somewhat resentful that no one recognizes their presence. But how could anyone, since ghosts don't really exist? Their tricks to gain attention, moaning and rattling chains, don't amount to much in a world inured to terrors. Now and then one will update his work and honk the car horn until the battery goes dead. No use. It's dismissed as curious but trivial, another of life's little irritations. They have a persistent feeling, never quite articulated, that one day they will awaken to life again. Like someone always on the verge of making it big. Something unspecific, winning the lottery perhaps, or an inheritance. When they manage to focus for an instant on a thought, the triumph of that instant becomes equated with the deed. As when, having duly noted that the cobwebs need to be cleaned from a particular corner, I proceed complacently to other activities. Centuries of woolgathering pass in what seems to them only moments. The earth changes until nothing is recognizable and still this vague longing moves upon the face of the deep.

BANANAS

"Bananas, badly cooked meat,
candy at the carnival,
or flies in conjunction with the heat
caused Joey Stoner to die of polio ...
or swimming in Skeleton Creek
with those nigger kids,"
old Mrs. Clark said, she seen him ...

You have to take care to prevent
slump shoulders, flat feet.
If the baby sleeps on his back
the back of his head will be flat.
One has to make constant small corrections,
keeping the time
and the position of the stars.

That light that comes to us
across billions of miles of space
is only a reminder
of something that happened a long time ago.
In the split-second before hydrogen formed,
when a decision was called for,
nobody did a thing.

Introspection and examination,
your own fooling and fussing,
pushes the electrons around
so when you return home late,
tiptoe down the hall, shoes in hand
suddenly there's a lampcord, a rollerskate ...

Outside, the summer insects
orbit the single light on the corner
and from far down the block
a child calls out in the dark
"You can't get me. You can't get me."

ON AGING

There are no compensations for growing old, certainly
not wisdom. And one gave up anticipating heaven long
ago. Perhaps there is a kind of anesthesia resulting from
short-term memory loss, from diminished libido, from
apathy and fatigue that is mistaken for patience.

The rich can afford to grow old gracefully but the flesh
of the poor shows each defeat like a photographic plate
that records the movement of the planets and the stars
and the rotation of the earth. Eyesight fails and hearing,
the skin wrinkles and cracks, the bones twist, the muscles
degenerate ... It takes all morning to open a can of soup.

The world collapses inward. Memory is no recompense.
The past is fiction, a story of interest only to the young.
There is only, as there always was, the moment. The
instant, which, when you become aware of it, is blinding
as the flash when someone snaps a picture of you blowing
out the candles.

RESTORATION

The idea is to restore one of these Victorian monsters to its original grandeur—with a modern kitchen and bathroom, of course. Low-cost home improvement loans are available.

In the old days things were built to last ... giant oak timbers imbedded in granite, cast iron cogwheels and worm gears that drove certain adjuncts of the heavenly spheres. Pieces remain but no one remembers exactly what they were for.

In those days fuel was cheap. One could heat several rooms with an afternoon of hard thought on the subject of free will. Inside one of the cupboards is a special small door to the outside, like a pet door, so the cold can come in.

With rotten timbers, plaster falling all around, this job requires a will of iron, like the border fence, bent and rusted near the ground, that still hangs on like God and empire. Let's paint this place in true colors of the period, dark green and red, repression and madness. An excess of quiet ostentatiousness.

WINTER CLOTHES

We come in puffing and stamping—goose down, wool, heavy boots, mittens, scarf...Winter clothes bear the same relationship to the body as the body does to the soul, a sort of cocoon where those you thought you knew are changed beyond recognition...We greet each other with awkward affection, like bears. Someone removes a glove and extends a pale hand.

His hand on the green silk of her dress, lightly, on the small of her back, sleepwalking there in the forest. And on the inside, the raveled thread ends, untidy windfall where the hunter walks to flush the startled bird...and afterwards silence...a handful of feathers, like letters from another woman found in a bank box after his death, casting a whole new light on the subject.

When you get to the end there is always one more thing. The mind insists that we live on after death whether we walk stiffly in bodies cold and drained of color or drift like tall columns of mist across the northern lakes, taller than we were in life but no more substantial.

We must look inside to find the answer, pulling the layers away like the leaves of an artichoke. And the answer is incorrect.

WIND CHIME

Eventually someone will get sick of this clatter and will tie up the strings or remove the whole contraption. This instrument was meant for subtler sounds, silence and overtones, only the hint of a breeze, days in which the phone does not ring even once, long afternoons that fade into twilight with a single star there in the bell-clear western sky. I sigh and lay the book aside ... But the wind is unrelenting. It must have been like this long ago, a single sound over and over until at last someone sitting alone in the early dark became aware of it and realized what it means to be alive.

Nice Fish

1995

CORKSCREW

The woman next door comes over to return a corkscrew. "Thanks for letting us use this. I'm sorry you couldn't make it to the party." I don't remember being invited to a party. I stand looking at the thing dumbly as she goes. I don't recognize it. This isn't my corkscrew. Well, I don't really own this or anything else, really. That has become more apparent to me as time goes by. This is just another thing that came to my door of its own volition, out of some instinctual urge perhaps, the way bees swarm into a tree, piling up, forming what seems to be a single living shape; or came by accident, the way the wind makes a dust devil out of dirt and straw, whatever is at hand. It careens across the field, picks up a newspaper, picks up a driver's license, picks up a college degree ... "Margaret, I'd like you to meet Louis. He's not the guy I was telling you about." "Really? Who are you then?"

INSECTS

Insects never worry about where they are. A mosquito is so dedicated to the pursuit of warm blood that it neglects the long-range plan. If a mosquito follows you into the house it waits patiently until the lights are out and you are nearly asleep then it heads straight for your ear. Suppose you miss, hit yourself in the head and knock yourself out and the mosquito succeeds in drawing blood. How will it get out of the house again to breed? What are its chances?

Insects don't seem to have a sense of place but require only a certain ambiance. A fly that gets driven 500 miles in a car and then is finally chased out the window does not miss the town where it spent its maggothood. Wherever this is it will be the same; a pile of dog shit, a tuna salad sandwich, a corpse.

THE LANGUAGE OF CROWS

A crow has discovered a scrap of roadkill on the blacktop and can't resist telling everyone in a loud voice. Immediately another crow arrives on the scene and the fight begins, cawing, flapping, and biting. Suddenly crows come flying in from every direction to enter the battle, skimming low over the treetops, all cawing loudly. Finally one of the crows makes off with the prize and flies a few hundred yards into the trees. But as soon as he stops the others are on him and the fight begins again. This scene is repeated time after time and each time the crows move farther away into the woods until their cawing has grown faint but remains undiminished in intensity. Then suddenly here they are again, full-force and in your face. Crows have a limited vocabulary, like someone who swears constantly, and communication seems to be a matter of emphasis and volume.

If you lie quietly in bed in the very early morning, in the half-light before time begins and listen carefully, the language of crows is easy to understand. "Here I am." That's really all there is to say and we say it again and again.

SPONTANEOUS COMBUSTION

As the late afternoon sunlight comes in through the window, one thing then another, a chair, a photograph, a glass on the table, is illuminated then fades as the sun moves on. It is as if a thought became suddenly conscious, a few words of an old song perhaps, "gaudeamus igitur something something ..." something you never understood but that remained with you anyway. It is that time when one is, finally, no longer a child but not yet old, full of strength and light, that passes so quickly, never to return. But then, who knows? After all it wasn't the young lovers ignited by passion, though there were rumors ... It was just an old man, no permanent address, wearing everything he owned, two old coats, worn trousers, three shirts, wool long johns and a hat. Perhaps it was the old clothes like oily rags and the irritation of wool on skin that set the spark. Some irritation, some annoyance. His soul rose above the flames like the ashy skeleton of a piece of newspaper still glittering at the edges, then broke apart, disappeared in the brisk March wind.

THE NIGHT ROOM

There is one bedroom in the east wing where it is always night. It is a favorite with the overworked rich and famous as a place to catch up on some much needed rest. Elizabeth Taylor spends a week of every year in the night room and Ed McMahon (or is it Dick Clark?) often comes here to vacation. The room is on the ground floor and has access to a private walled garden which was added in the 16th century after the unusual properties of the room were discovered. If you open the curtains you can see the moonlight reflected on the water in the little fountain or the stars shining above the garden wall even though it may be noon on a sunny day. It would be curious to see into the room from the garden, if that were possible, to watch the room's current occupant, perhaps reading by lamplight or asleep, a shadowy form on the bed, unaware that it is now nearly three in the afternoon. And if awakened he or she would, no doubt, see you the same way, as a shadowy form between the hibiscus and the lemon verbena, possibly dangerous.

DRIP

Water does not want to be still. The ocean rages in its bed even though there is nowhere to go. Down, always down. When a fissure opens in the ground water pours in. On to the center of the earth!

Water has come to a halt here in the swamp. Stymied. All life here eventually ends up as muck under the water. You can reach down and bring up a hundred years in a single handful; the substance of things hoped for.

Water does not want to be contained. Silently, secretly, water feels along the walls of the pipe for a flaw, seeks the misthreaded joint, the faulty faucet ... The drips go orderly, joyfully into the sink counting the seconds of the long night.

WINTER LIGHT

The sun glitters at a low angle through the bare trees, a distant January sun, light without warmth, making a pattern of stripes, varied widths of sunlight and shadow, across the road. The car moves like a scanner over a bar code. This is the tally of a very protracted shopping trip. Light and dark, light and dark ... It's the old duality: good and evil, male and female, dogs and cats, etc. The strobe light flashes of sun are hypnotic, dangerous, creating the illusion that the car is stopped and that the road is no more than a series of still photographs projected on a screen ... or the opposite illusion—that you've been somewhere, that you are on your way somewhere.

AFTER SCHOOL

She had made a kind of promise to herself not to stop, but his house was right on her way home, besides, she thought, it was OK because they were just friends, they had always been just friends ... But, of course, he wasn't home when she knocked and his mother seemed like she was in a bad mood or something, but then his mother often seemed to be in a bad mood. Now it was nearly dark. Lights were on in some of the houses. The last sunlight shone red and orange on the bare birch trees and on the snowdrifts. It was beautiful, perfectly still, almost like a painting, she thought. And she was the one in the picture, walking home after school, always, toward supper and the long winter night.

YOUR BABY

Cry and curse, stamp your foot down hard, because the surface of the earth is no more than a crust, a bunch of loose tectonic plates, something like the bones of a baby's skull, floating on a core of molten magma: chaos and anarchy, the fires of hell. And as you've been told repeatedly, it's all in your hands. It's like the egg you were given in Marriage and Family class. "This is your baby, take care of it." So dutifully you drew a smile face on, then as an afterthought added a pair of eyebrows shaped like rooftops. It gave the egg baby a slightly sinister appearance. Then a friend added Dracula fangs and said, "See it looks just like its daddy." "Let me see" someone said and gave your elbow a shove ...

Late at night. Where is your demon child now, as you sit dozing over the periodic tables?

THE GATE

The gate makes a few hesitant moves in the wind, some false starts that allow a few dry leaves to blow into the yard. Then as if suddenly determined to leave forever, the gate swings wide open, bounces off a snow bank and slams shut. It remains still for a time, as if stunned by the experience. Then it begins again, moving a few tentative inches before the big rush. The gate is teased by the wind. It's useless. The gate is set in its ways. It can only break at the hinges, splinter and fall down.

WEST WIND

Trees fling themselves about in order to evict the noisy birds. A little boy leans into the wind and runs. He wants to fly with the crows. He flaps his arms and squawks. Mother is determined, runs after, grabs him and straps him into the stroller seat. "You stay right here." The little boy wants to fly like the wrapper from a hamburger, all brightly colored, into the busy sky.

So many plans, but the stakes are broken, the string knotted and tangled. Yet I feel a sense of accomplishment. I hold my car keys in my hand and it seems to me that I have just returned from a long trip.

HOW TO TELL A WOLF FROM A DOG

A wolf carries his head down, tail down. He has a look of preoccupation, or worry, you might think. He has a family to support. He probably has a couple of broken ribs from trying to bring down a moose. He's not getting workman's comp, either and no praise for his efforts. The wolf looks unemployed, flat broke.

On the other hand, a dog of similar features, a husky or a malamute, has his head up, ears up, looks attentive, self-confident, cheerful and obedient. He is fully employed with an eye toward promotion. He carries his tail high, like a banner. He's part of a big organization and has the title of "man's best friend."

ANGELS

Contrary to popular belief angels have no important function in the array of mythic beings. They seem to be primarily decorative, hovering above a saint pierced with arrows or part of a heavenly chorus, white and shining in the sky. They are like yachts skimming the blue, so beautiful in the sun. Useless as guardians or messengers, they have a lot of time on their hands. One has lingered too long among humans, fascinated by the possibility of a toothache or unrequited love. Heedless that his wings will no longer lift him more than a foot or so off the ground, one shuffles down the street at dusk, pretending to be a nineteenth century poet, a misunderstood genius, hunched over in his great cape.

FREEWAY

Just south of Hinckley a car passes me from behind. I glance over at the driver. It's my old girlfriend from 25 years ago! Exactly the same, she hasn't aged a day. The same blond, windblown and frazzled hair, the same intent look. She's on her way back to Oklahoma probably, all her stuff loaded inside. She's on her way to get some money out of her ex, or to some other desperate appointment that will finally make the difference. Whatever I'm into now, whatever I've become, she doesn't want to know. She won't look at me. She knows that you can't take your eyes off the road for even an instant.

CAMPSITE

He paddles the canoe across the still water, alone in the evening, back to his camp. The water is perfect for walking, flat as the floor of a ballroom. This evening only the shadows of spruce and pine walk out from the forest, a time of darkening reflection. He pulls the canoe onto the shore and turns it over in just the way that his ancestors did. He builds a fire the way they did except that he uses matches and a few pieces of newspaper. He does not speak. His ancestors did not speak. They could only grunt and point. He does not know who his ancestors were except that they, like him, were notorious liars. He sits in a circle of light. An owl calls out from the trees. He sits in the smoke and pokes at the glowing coals with a stick. He moves a little to the left. The smoke follows him. He moves a little to the right.

SAINTHOOD

Because of my extraordinary correctness and sensitivity of late I have been elevated to the status of Temporary Minor Saint (secular). The position comes with a commendation praising my "uncharacteristic reticence tantamount to sagacity." This means that my entire being is now suffused with a pale radiance somewhat like the light from a small fluorescent bulb, the light on a kitchen range perhaps, only not quite so bright, and that instead of walking I now float at an altitude of approximately three inches above the ground. I move about at a slow and stately speed as befits my new rank. I move to the left or right by inclining my head and upper body in the appropriate direction. It's a less-than-perfect condition. The light keeps my wife awake at night and though the added height is beneficial, moving about in a crowd presents difficulties. My forward speed seems to be fixed and, though slow, it's quite tricky to stop. I lean back but momentum carries me forward like a boat. Suddenly turning my head can send me veering into the person next to me or into a wall. In order to remain in one place I've found it necessary to attach cords to my belt on one end and to various solid objects around the room on the other. These days I take my meals standing up, tethered like the Hindenburg.

THE VIEW FROM SCOVILLE POINT

This is not the end, but you can see the end from here. Well, often when you think you have come to the end there is one more thing. Out there is a scattering of islands some thick with spruce and balsam, marshes and bogs. Easy to get bogged down with last minute details. It's better to think of each island as a stepping-stone. Flag Island, South Government, North Government, Merritt Island, and last of all Passage Island with its light, not the light at the end of the tunnel, not the warm encompassing light, just a brief flash and then ... it comes again. Beyond all are the open waters of the big lake ... Each passenger receives a hug, a bouquet of flowers, a small box of candy.

SNOW HOLLOWS

That's where he sleeps, that ne'er-do-well half-brother of yours, in the snow hollow, that patch of dry ground on the south side of the big spruce tree, where the branches hang down, heavy with snow, a place protected from the wind and weather. Somewhat. In a few days he'll move to another place much like this one. Each time one of those trees bends down to touch his head a little more gray appears in his hair. Well, what did he expect? He thinks the world owes him a living. Now and then the winds blow his way—bringing a page of yesterday's newspaper. He's out there now in the blue afternoon gloom with his great expectations, his moose call and that ridiculous hunting knife with its fringed leather scabbard. Let him stay out there.

THE CURE FOR WARTS

Draw a circle in red around the wart while repeating the incantation, words not to be spoken aloud in the presence of another human being. Once those words are spoken they are forever changed and you must begin again. A few special words to say to yourself in the silence and the dark. A phrase to worry over, polish and perfect, to believe in, despite all evidence to the contrary. In a few weeks the wart should drop off. But magic is so approximate. Perhaps only a wheel cover comes loose from your car as you drive down the interstate and rolls into the ditch. No chance of retrieving it in the heavy traffic. Later perhaps one of the ubiquitous crows will spot it there in the high grass and fly down to admire his reflection in the shiny surface. Beautiful. Fascinating. He opens his beak to sing. Yes, perhaps he'll sing.

THE MIND READER

He says, "The mind leaps the way a salmon flashes in the air. So quick you think you might have imagined it. The mind leaps to protect its darkest secret thus giving it away. But that is of no interest to me. What I need to know is the date of birth or the number of keys on the key ring."

Tonight the mind reader has retired early with a blond woman he met at the show, the one with the "interesting mind." On the bedside table with the watch and wallet is his hidden communication device. If you put the tiny earpiece to your ear you can hear a faint sound, like the sound of the sea, the distant hiss and crackle of the autonomic nervous system

NO HIRED MAN

It turns out that everything I've written is untrue. It wasn't entirely innocent. For instance, when I described a woman kneeling down near the creek, I knew that it wasn't a woman but a pile of brush, a few rags and some shreds of polyvinyl. Worse. When I think about it now I realize that there was no brush pile. No creek, either.

One evening after supper, when I was three or four years old, the hired man said "I'll make you something." He took a couple of brazing rods from the welder and spent a long time twisting them together with pliers. I tried to wait patiently. Then suddenly he said, "It won't work" and threw the thing on the pile of scrap metal outside the garage. After he had gone, walking the long road to town, I looked at the thing he'd made. I carried it around for a while then put it back on the scrap heap. I never found out what he intended to make. Or what it was.

Just Above Water

1997

ONE

THE FISHING LURE

I've spent a great deal of my life fretting over things that most people wouldn't waste their time on. Trying to explain things I haven't a clue about. It's given me that worried look, that wide-eyed, staring look. The look that wild animals sometimes have, deer for instance, standing in the middle of the highway trying to make sense of the situation: "What *is* that?" Motionless, transfixed. The same look that's on the face of the fishing lure. Stupidity? Terror? What is the right bait for these conditions? High cirrus clouds, cold front moving in. It's all a trick anyway. What is this thing supposed to be? A minnow? A bug? Gaudy paint and hooks all over. It's like bleached blond hair and bright red lipstick. Nobody *really* believes it. There isn't a way in the world I'd bite on that thing. But I might swim in just a little closer.

SHIPS

Now that the children are grown and their divorces are final some of my friends have moved into smaller shells somewhere up the shore. As for me, I still enjoy being all at sea, an intimate of the luminous life of the deep, bobbing up and down among ships that pass in the night, keeping my head just above water. But I don't worry, I know I'll get back to sleep when the morning fog comes in, when the Pacific fleet arrives, ghost ships from the Coral Sea. They come in silently and never cough or shuffle their feet but I know they're in the room, great hulking shapes, old and unpleasant relatives, the color of the sea, the color of the sky, gathered around my bed.

SMALL FISH

He's too small to keep so I remove the hook and put him back in the water. He hesitates a moment near the surface, as if not quite realizing where he is, then with a swift movement of the tail he's gone. He's back in it now, his own deep blue-green, the daily hunger and panic. He has no way of thinking about this experience. He was, then he was not, and now he is again. A seizure. But then, moments later, he's back on the surface a few feet from the boat, lying on his side, the gills working, one in the water, one in the useless air. He'd hit the bait hard and the hook had gone in deep—youthful folly, you could say, or extreme hunger, or plain bad luck. I reach out and try to grab him, but he's still too quick even in this condition. He swims down again. He's determined but the water will not have him any more. In a few seconds he's back, farther from the boat, in the domain of sunlight and hungry seagulls.

THE INEFFABLE

Most of my life I was not paying attention, I think. That's why I remember so little—the names of lovers and intimate friends, forgotten ... the houses I lived in, the kinds of cars I drove. What was I thinking about, then? The ineffable, of course—I was trying to capture the ineffable. The way a person might set a live trap and catch a skunk. What now? It's a difficult situation. Certainly not the stay against confusion Frost talked about. I've heard a lot of skunk stories, and it seems to me that they all have unfortunate and ridiculous endings: baths in tomato juice and buried clothing. One story involved dynamite in the crawl space beneath a house. I believe that the person in the story was a great-uncle of mine.

SPRING BREAK-UP

Out on the big lake it's all glitter and surface, rumor and innuendo, voices that run like a shiver, out and out ... At the shore great slabs of ice pile up: ruined glass houses, the speculative mansions of heaven that just didn't sell and fell prey to vandals. Wherever two worlds come together damage is done. Yet the world of dreams is not much different than our own. In both one accepts cruelty and nonsense gratefully and believes. Even if you place your feet carefully and expect the worst, awakening is as sudden and unreckoned as the water.

A PATCH OF OLD SNOW

Here's a patch of snow nestled in the roots of a spruce tree. A spot the sun never touches. Mid-May and there's still snow in the woods. It's startling to come upon this old snow on such a warm day. The record of another time. It's like coming across a forgotten photograph of yourself. The stylish clothes of the period look silly now. And your haircut! Awful. You were young, wasteful, selfish, completely mistaken and, probably, no less aware than today.

THE ANT HILL

On a hill overlooking the city an ant colony has come to life again now that the snow has melted. I watch the ants and make the obvious comparisons. There are workers and soldiers. There are crews clearing debris from entrances and passageways. There are ants who struggle with grass blades and sticks, objects that are much too large for them. There are others who do nothing at all except run around frantically waving their antennae. Administrators. But comparisons only go so far. No joy, no grief, no regret ... Apart from team spirit, it seems, the only emotional content is what we bring. If we had anything more substantial to offer, workers would surround it, as they have the corpse of this spider, and drag it down into the dark nursery.

BOREDOM

Nowadays I am seldom bored. There simply isn't time. Not because I am so busy, it's just that time passes more quickly as one gets older. Boredom that once lasted hours is now compacted, concentrated, so that one can experience hours of boredom in a few seconds. Intense boredom that causes one to nod off ... But only for five minutes. Or has it been an hour? Well, time is relative. Like that distant relative who used to be me, plodding home after school in a daydream, in a fog, so that each time he wakes he finds himself standing on the same red ant hill or running, side aching, breathless, for miles in the wrong direction with the murderous Willard brothers right behind.

MOTEL

The motel is very modern with fireproof doors and a sprinkler system and smoke alarms in every room. Each room has cable television with HBO. When you turn on the light in the bathroom a noisy exhaust fan comes on also. Screwed to the wall above the bed is a framed print of an old barn. Out in the hallway a faint odor of chlorine drifts up from the pool area. One of the steel doors slams shut and some children run shouting down the hall causing the entire prefabricated concrete third floor to shake. The couple in 312 are trying to get some sleep but there is a party going on in room 310. The loud talk goes on past midnight, who did what with whom and what she said and something about the real estate business (it seems they are all in the real estate business) then laughter. The motel is the last thing at the edge of town. If you slide open the opaque bathroom window you can see beyond the parking lot to an unused pasture where some papers have caught in the fence.

JUNE

It has been raining for three days, a slow unrelenting rain; east wind, 43 degrees. An average day. The goose stands in the yard with his head under his wing. Fishing is impossible and we have no money to go shopping. The only thing left is the life of the mind. We're desperate. Rain drums on the bottom of the canoe but the message eludes us, slips away with the water that runs into ditches and creeks, over rotted wood and rusted metal, down to the big lake, where the view is water, water and watery sky, and our toes touch only water.

LAUNDROMAT

Here you are again at the laundromat late Sunday evening. There are others here: the college student with his book, the woman in tight jeans, the mother with her noisy baby. It's not like the women gathered at the river, laughing and singing. This isn't a social occasion. Everyone seems bored, exhausted, anxious to finish the wash and go home. You're here now because of poor planning. This could have been done at a more congenial time. Well, how far ahead should one plan? Next week, next year, the next ice age ... ? Hard to believe but this is your real life, right now, watching the laundry go around. Something like watching television. And you are the star of the show, of course. Or maybe you aren't. Maybe you are only here as atmosphere, something peripheral, leading to a vague feeling of disappointment.

A WALK IN THE WOODS

Out here in the woods I can say anything I like without fear of contradiction. I am not faced with solving any of the great problems. I have only to cross a twenty-acre patch of mixed hardwoods and spruce from one road to another without getting lost. Really, I am as free as the birds that flit from tree to tree, like the nuthatch or the white-throated sparrow, singing "old Sam Peabody, Peabody, Peabody." Here the trees are doing their usual dance—arms extended, fingertips raised, feet firmly planted, swaying from side to side. Just across the clearing there's a group of slender aspen, all in their spring party dresses, chattering away. Now the music begins again. "Moon River." Ladies choice. That tall homely one bends over to whisper to her friend and... oh, hell, they're all looking straight at me.

SPRING WIND

The spring wind comes through and knocks over trash cans and trees. It has something to do with warm fronts and cold fronts, I think, or with high and low pressure systems, things that I don't really understand and that aren't really an explanation anyway. Ultimately the spring wind is the result of some relationship between the earth and the sun that may not be all that healthy, after all. The wind comes in a big huff, slams doors, pushes things around and kicks up the dirt. The big bully spring wind comes through on its way nowhere and, ha ha! We love it.

SAINTS

As soon as the snow melts the grass begins to grow. Even though the daytime high is barely above freezing, even though May is very like November, marsh marigolds bloom in the swamp and the popple trees produce a faint green that hangs under the low clouds like a haze over the valley. This is the way the saints live, no complaints, no suspicion, no surprise. If it rains carry an umbrella, if it's cold wear a jacket.

TWO

THREE A.M.

The god of three a.m. is the god of the dripping faucet, sirens, and barking dogs. He's been given titular charge of circumstances that cannot be controlled. "It's out of my hands," he says, repeatedly. He is a minor functionary, a troll that lives under a bridge. On the far side are the pastures of night where bright stars graze in the dark matter of the cosmos. He is fond of philosophic thought. "Of course, our understanding is limited. All we can do is adhere to those laws and principles that have been proven, time and again, to work." It seems there is some discrepancy in my papers. "A minor delay," he assures me. Now it's almost four.

STONE ARCH, NATURAL ROCK FORMATION

It is higher, more narrow, more treacherous than we imagined. And here we are in a spot where there's no going back, a point of no return. It has become too dangerous to continue as we have. We simply are not as sure-footed and nimble as we were when we started out. There's nothing to do but sit down, carefully, straddling the rock. Once seated, I'm going to turn slightly and hand the bag of groceries back to you. Then I'm going to scoot ahead a few inches and turn again. If you then lean forward carefully and hand me the bag you will be able to move ahead to the spot I previously occupied. It is a miserably slow process and we still have the problem of the steep descent on the other side. But if we are patient, my love, I believe we will arrive safely on the ground again a few yards from where we began.

BEAUTIFUL CHILD

People exclaim "What a pretty little girl!" But whenever a stranger speaks to her, she buries her face in her mother's lap or puts on a frown, looks away and refuses to answer. When she is alone, she sings a little song. She pushes back her long blond hair. She pretends to be a ballerina or perhaps the lady on the tight rope high above an audience that is invisible there in the dark. As she takes her first delicate step into the spotlight the crowd breaks into applause ... Years later her boyfriend asks, "What's wrong tonight?" They have walked far down the beach and it occurs to him that she is angry. "Did I do something?" It's a question he asks frequently. "It's nothing," she says. Then there is a long silent moment. "You wouldn't understand." She looks far away across the water.

BELIEF

We all have certain things we believe in. Usually they don't amount to much. Some people believe that if you put a spoon in the open bottle champagne will keep its fizz. Others believe that hot water will freeze faster than cold or that when you flush a toilet in the southern hemisphere the water always turns clockwise. Some people believe that you should wear a beanie and others believe in funny collars. In the absence of anything better these beliefs serve to separate your life from others lurking in the forest around you, like scent marking. People have certain phrases they like to use. *At the end of the day...* or *... on the same page...* and words such as *paradigm, trope, facilitator, objecthood...* words that don't mean anything. We drop them like breadcrumbs to mark the way home— where we all intend to return one day.

THE SPEAKER

The speaker points out that we don't really have much of a grasp of things, not only the big things, the important questions, but the small everyday things. "How many steps up to your front door? What kind of tree grows in your back yard? What is the name of your district representative? What is your wife's shoe size? Can you tell me the color of your sweetheart's eyes? Do you remember where you parked the car?" The evidence is overwhelming. Most of us never truly experience life. "We drift through life in a daydream, missing the true *richness* and *joy* that life has to offer." When the speaker has finished we gather around to sing a few inspirational songs. You and I stand at the back of the group and hum along since we have forgotten most of the words.

YELLOW HAT

Nobody knows what will happen, what catastrophes, what miraculous transformations. In order to maintain faith, to plan for the future, the world must be simplified. Here is the window out of which you can see a tree, a bright red flower, green grass extending over the hill. On top of the hill, yes, there I am ... two legs, two arms, ten fingers like sausages and a smile on my big round face. And just six inches above my yellow hat the blue sky begins.

CROWS AT DUSK

Just before dusk a crow lands near the top of the tall white pine on a bare branch, adjusts himself, turning one way then another, and is still. In a few moments another crow joins him. They greet each other with a kind of low croaking noise and touching of beaks. Then they are silent, hunkered down, feathers ruffled slightly, side by side on the branch. The lake has taken on the idea of silence. Silence, night coming on, sleep. Suddenly, without any indication of his intention, the first crow rouses himself and flies away. The second sits alone for a moment or two then flies also, in a different direction.

TIME

For no apparent reason my wristwatch, which is lying on the bedside table, suddenly begins to tick louder. As if it wanted my attention. What is it? What could a watch possibly want? Cleaning? A new battery? Or is it time calling attention to itself. It wants ... something, *tempus fugit*, and all that. It's a big semi-domestic animal, confused from so long with humans, like a big dog that whines to be let out and barks to be let back in. It doesn't know what it wants anymore than we do. Want to go for a walk big boy? Yeah, yeah! He pulls us around with leash. First one way then another. It's a constant tug-of-war. He wants to be turned loose, to run around in circles sniffing at everything. He doesn't care if you come too. If you can keep up.

THE CANOE

Of the things I own I like my canoe best, I think. So light-weight and easy to portage. Delicate, it seems, fragile as memory, but really it's quite strong. Eighteen feet long, it will carry two, sometimes three, adults and their gear, and it's amazing the amount of baggage people bring. Even fully loaded with only a few inches of freeboard, the canoe moves gracefully over the water. Remarkably stable given the circumstance. It can handle most whitewater but I don't need whitewater. The river at its best, single-minded and self-righteous, is enough. I like it when the river flows straight and silvery for half a mile or more before it bends and disappears in the trees.

AFTER THE STORM

The stream is in turmoil today, running bank-full with brown, muddy water, making a terrible roar, an echo of last night's thunderstorm. Despite the water's headlong rush there's a lot of uncertainty here. The surrounding forest is silent, depressed, saturated and dripping beneath an overcast sky. A piece of a tree limb, probably broken off in the storm, has fallen into the river and is stalled in one of the pools above the falls. It bumps around in the foam-covered eddies and back-currents, slowly circling, snagging occasionally on the rocks, looking awkward and confused, like an adolescent confronted finally with the adult world. The stick is bullied and pushed by the water. Then chance sends the branch out into the main current and it bolts downstream like a frightened animal. As if a split-second decision had been made. As if there was a choice in this matter.

THE SEWING MACHINE

When she sat down in the morning to sew she discovered that her machine was completely out of adjustment. Obviously someone had gotten in during the night and fooled around with it. One afternoon she sat down on the couch for only a minute or two. Then something caused her to wake with a start. There was a man sitting right next to her! Her waking caused him to wake also. When he saw her he got up and out of there in a hurry! Locks were no good though she had them changed twice. She began blocking the doors by wedging a chair under the doorknob of each. That was a problem whenever she passed out—once she lay there on the kitchen floor for an hour before the police were able to break in. The police. A lot of good they were. Criminals loose all over town. What could an old woman do alone, trapped inside her house?

AUGUST EVENING

A cloud of tiny insects hovers just above the edge of the point where the land drops away steeply to the lake. There must be a thousand of them flying every which way in a sexual frenzy. Yet the cloud keeps its integrity. It's the world's largest singles bar! There's some selection process at work here. It's obvious that not just anyone will do. But it works. Mated pairs, tail-to-tail, drop out of the cloud, sinking together to the ground. The weight of it brings them down while the others continue the dance, round and round in the warm evening air.

UPON THE WATERS

After a week of gray skies a single shaft of sunlight breaks through the clouds over the lake and illuminates a small area of the surface water with the holy faith, inaccessible to those of us on shore. When the Manistee began to break up, the sailors took the only door that opened and went down.

Thirty fathoms down fish patrol the slimy wreckage, and rise quickly into the light, into the commingling of water and air. As quickly as that, in that moment your attention focused somewhere out there, the baby drifted away. His diaper changed, his bottle filled, he rides the waves in his basket like a king, slightly annoyed and a bit uncomfortable.

DRINKING POEM

Because I have no one else
to drink with tonight
I go down to the lakeshore
and take the water
and the moon for my companions.
Already the moon is high
and the water, stirred by the wind,
becomes loquacious.
It's the same old story.
The water sculpts these rocks.
It takes a thousand years,
smoothing and polishing.
There's no money in it,
so far from the major markets.
As I listen I grow drowsy.
Water on the rocks ...
What's to be done?
What's to be done?

THREE

SEPTEMBER

for Phil Dentinger

One evening the breeze blowing in the window turns cold and you pull the blankets around you. The leaves of the maples along Wallace Avenue have already turned red and someone you loved does not come around anymore. That's all right, you tell yourself, things change with the cycle of the seasons and evolve. A mistake, a wrong turn takes you somewhere else, someplace new.

But perhaps there are forces other than chance at work here. Perhaps a person changes deliberately out of boredom with the present condition. Perhaps our children, from a desire to become simply other than what we are, grow feathers, learn to breathe underwater or to see in the dark.

PERSONAL HISTORY

One has a feeling of having not lived life to its fullest, having not really accomplished anything and at the same time there is a feeling of regret for past sins, those things one would like to undo. And all the while the years passing, passing ... turning to decades, centuries. Think of the Hittites, at one point the hottest power in the world, a practical, down-to-earth people but one that did little, finally, to advance human civilization. What would a Hittite say if you met on the street?

"Listen, I'd like to apologize for those unwanted advances I made."

"That's all right. It was a long time ago."

"Nevertheless, I feel uneasy about it. It was rude and selfish of me. It's just that you were so. . . ."

"It's OK, really. I can honestly say I never think of it."

THE WAVES

The east wind has risen today and the waves rise up. Praise to all rising up! To the life that seemed might never return after so many days of dead calm. The wind sends wave after wave scudding toward the shore where the ragged grass clings to the rock. Waves. I recognize some of them. They lift from the void, white-haired but determined, as if each had a purpose, a private destiny, someplace to go. (Brunch? A board meeting?) Once the savior walked across the water to give each wave a hand up. Perhaps he is returning even now, but the road to the shore is long, long ... The waves break and fall face forward, losing touch, losing credibility, losing all pretense of dignity.

GRAVITY

It turns out that the drain pipe from the sink is attached to nothing and water just runs right onto the ground in the crawl space underneath the house and then trickles out into the stream that passes through the back yard. It turns out that the house is not really attached to the ground but sits atop a few loose concrete blocks all held in place by gravity, which, as I understand it, means "seriousness." Well, this is serious enough. If you look into it further you will discover that the water is not attached to anything either and that perhaps the rocks and the trees are not all that firmly in place. The world is a stage. But don't try to move anything. You might hurt yourself, besides that's a job for the stagehands and union rules are strict. You are merely a player about to deliver a soliloquy on the septic system to a couple dozen popple trees and a patch of pale blue sky.

AUTUMN

Black crows wheeling overhead ... the shocking blue sky above the gold leaf autumn trees.

It's one of those roads that starts off purposefully but most likely trails off into a jumble of popple and alder. Remember this is hunting season, bullets flying everywhere. Best to sing or shout as you go along.

This world we love and cannot hold, this world we love and mistreat, that mistreats us, that crumbles at a touch, that drifts away like smoke ...

There are sounds out of our range, too high, too low. There is light beyond the visible spectrum. Our brains are unable to make sense of our own lives. And my hair goes every which way.

It's a bad system. Who's responsible for this mess anyway? Jenkins. I recognize the plodding style.

SOME NOTES ON WRITING

Contrary to the pronouncements of certain notable poets it makes no difference whether you write with a pencil or a pen. Notebooks are another matter. You will find that in certain notebooks less than half the pages are of any use, others must be abandoned almost immediately. There's no useful formula. Notebooks are a matter of trial and error.

You sit woodenly at the table, notebook open, pencil near at hand awaiting the arrival of the muse. Because you are staring into the middle distance you haven't noticed that the muse has already flown into the room and hangs as if suspended by monofilament, twisting slightly in the warm air currents. In order to come beneath her hand that is outstretched in blessing it may be necessary to move your table to another part of the room.

Brother bear has caught cold and gone to sleep in his den. Brother fox is rummaging in the fallen leaves for airline tickets. Everybody and his brother is going about his business. No one is waiting for you to finish this but where else will you live?

THE LIFE OF THE POET

I once believed that behind all the things I did, or more often, failed to do, there was a great moral purpose, or at least some coherent principle, a *raison d'être*. If there is such a principle it has never become quite clear to me. Instead, over the years, I have managed to take a random selection of bad habits and herd them together into a life. Also, in order to disguise my absolute laziness I have mastered the age-old art of appearing to be productive when, actually, this is the only thing I'm doing. (Republicans suspected as much all along.) Someone comes up to my desk and I get busy scribbling, totally preoccupied. "What? Oh, I'm sorry ..." In my haste to appear industrious I find I have written: "and herd them together into a *wife*."

THE BOOK

Every night I read the same paragraph, the words of fire, the perfect symmetry! But it is impossible to hold. My eyes close and the book falls from my hands ... Sometime later in the night I wake, long enough to switch off the lamp and pull the blankets around me. By morning I've forgotten everything. Outside a gray workday drizzle is falling and the text is flat, uninspired. At night on the page between awake and asleep, the world makes perfect sense. There we meet again for the first time and you take my hand.

THE COUPLE

They no longer sleep quite as well as they did when they were younger. He lies awake thinking of things that happened years ago, turning uncomfortably from time to time, pulling on the blankets. She worries about money. First one and then the other is awake during the night, in shifts as if keeping watch, though they can't see very much in the dark and it's quiet. They are sentries at some outpost, an abandoned fort somewhere in the middle of the Great Plains where only the wind is a regular visitor. Each stands guard in the wilderness of an imagined life in which the other sleeps untroubled.

THE SKIFF

Jim was at the tiller holding her into the wind, moving us along while I lifted the net. Then we began to drift. The net was damn near to pull my arms off and I thought damnit Jim, pay attention to what the hell you're doing. I turned my head to yell at him and he wasn't there! I dropped the net, scrambled back past the engine compartment and grabbed the tiller, all the while looking around like crazy to see if I could spot Jim's head above the waves ... but there was nothing, not even a gull, just a few clouds far away on the eastern horizon. I circled back along the net yelling my head off. I cut the engine to listen. The quiet was strange after the engine noise, the sound of the waves lapping against the hull. Not much of a wind, two-foot waves, just a breeze out of the southwest. It seemed impossible. I must have spent hours going around in circles, calling out, even after I knew it was useless. There was nothing, no sign. Nothing but water and sky. It must have been the water took him, but for all I know it was the sky. Then I noticed the half peanut butter sandwich on the seat beside me. It startled me as if it had been a snake. There was a bite out of one end. Jim's jacket was gone. That sandwich was the only thing to prove Jim had ever been here at all.

BONES

The leaves have fallen, the geese have flown south and your hair has turned gray. Most of the people who knew you when you were a baby are dead now. Whatever it was caused them to stand up and walk around as if they knew where they were going has flown also. Something caused them to hesitate, turn back to the house, then begin again slamming the screen door behind. That impulse has gone. Nothing remains now but bones, the skeptical bones. Soon snow will come to cover them again. No one has coffee ready, there are no fields to plow and they know all about you, shuffling around in the dry leaves. "It's only that kid up there, no reason to get up."

THE HERMIT OF FOX FARM ROAD

Perhaps one's existence is dependent on the recognition of that existence by others. One ceases to be because one is no longer perceived. Like the tree that falls in the forest that makes a noise only if there are ears to hear. If the human attention span were longer people would live longer lives. The way we are, we can hold a concept for only a brief period. Then our minds wander, we become bored. We want something new on the Top Forty. Yet it seems to me that I am still here—so perhaps she remembers, (no one else would) though we spoke only a few times and nothing I tried to say came out right. Only dimly now she imagines what I am, a stick figure, nearly invisible among the sticks of these woods.

NOVEMBER AGAIN

November again and the snow comes sudden and heavy. This is what we like best. This is what we paid our money for. Snow on snow, all day and all night, everything muffled, distant. Tomorrow, no school, no work, no worship service, no visitation of the sick, the poor, the widows or the orphans. Whatever it was nothing can be done about it now. Your old position has been filled. Your footsteps have been filled. The roads are filled, drifted shut. Finally, even the directions are obliterated in the heavy snowfall.

DECEMBER

These winter days are so short, pale, a lingering twilight between the long nights, a scrap of paper shoved under the door into a dark apartment. A note, a thinly veiled threat perhaps: "Only ten shopping days 'til Christmas." No, something else. What can be said in such a small space? Outside, the streetlights are coming on. "I was able to get here at last. Sorry to have missed you."

FOUR

TOO MUCH SNOW

Unlike the Eskimos we only have one word for snow but we have a lot of modifiers for that word. There is too much snow, which, unlike rain, does not immediately run off. It falls and stays for months. Someone wished for this snow. Someone got a deal, five cents on the dollar, and spent the entire family fortune. It's the simple solution. It covers everything. We are never satisfied with the arrangement of the snow so we spend hours moving the snow from one place to another. Too much snow. I box it up and send it to family and friends. I send a big box to my cousin in California and one to Uncle Ralph in Texas. I send a small box to my mother. She writes, "Don't send so much. I'm all alone now, I'll never be able to use so much." To you I send a single snowflake, beautiful, complex and delicate: different from all the others.

JACK B. NIMBLE

The only light is the light you carry. You can feel the darkness coming up close behind. If you turn suddenly the darkness jumps back, the way the lion retreats momentarily from the desperate wildebeest. Once you were a beacon. Once you set the candlestick atop your head and did the rumba, the cha cha, the limbo, until the wee hours of the morning. You hold that candle so carefully in front of you that it makes strange shadows and lines across your face but, honestly, I've never seen you looking better. And that new suit, I think, works wonders.

THE WORKING LIFE

Unless you have a boss who is really a jerk, the job is a minor discomfort, like shoes that are just a bit too tight. Most of us go through our workdays mechanically without thinking about what we are doing. "Hello. Anybody in there?" Our minds are elsewhere. "Hello, hello" the burglar calls out. Nobody home. You've become part of the vast, undulating daydream, swaying in the wind like prairie grass. The burglar breaks the pathetic lock, empties the contents of the drawers, pulls the books from the shelves ... There's your whole life strewn across the floor. The burglar steals the TV and the stereo and in return leaves new Visa and Mastercards with your name on them. You won't know this until hours later. This time of year we go to work in darkness, return home in darkness.

A PLACE FOR EVERYTHING

It's so easy to lose track of things. A screwdriver, for instance. "Where did I put that? I had it in my hand just a minute ago." You wander vaguely from room to room, having forgotten, by now, what you were looking for; staring into the refrigerator, the bathroom mirror ..."I really could use a shave ..."

Some objects seem to disappear immediately while others never want to leave. Here is a small black plastic gizmo with a serious demeanor that turns up regularly, like a politician at public functions. It seems to be an "integral part," a kind of switch with screw holes so that it can be attached to something larger. Nobody knows what. It probably went with something that was thrown away years ago. This thing's use has been forgotten but it looks so important that we are afraid to throw it in the trash. It survives by bluff, like certain insects that escape being eaten because of their formidable appearance.

My father owned a large, three-bladed, brass propeller that he saved for years. Its worth was obvious, it was just that it lacked an immediate application since we didn't own a boat and lived hundreds of miles from any large bodies of water. The propeller survived all purges and cleanings, living, like royalty, a life of lonely privilege, mounted high on the garage wall.

ICE

Walking on the icy pavement demands your attention. You have to learn to read the color, the texture, learn where you can safely step, learn to watch for the smooth, almost invisible ice or ice hidden by a light dusting of snow—suddenly you're flat on your back. Children don't worry about it. Their bodies are flexible and resilient and they have a shorter distance to fall. They fall, jump up and continue running. It's nothing. If a person of my age and size falls it makes a considerable impact. It's painful and embarrassing. Once I fell in front of the hardware store downtown, just like that, both feet straight out in front of me. Passersby gave me a strange look, not concern, more like disbelief. "What is this guy doing?" The very old, women on high-risk shopping trips, old men shoveling snow on rooftops, seem to have forgotten the ice entirely. If their frail bodies were caught by the least wind they would skitter and clatter over the hard surface for miles.

PARADISE

January finally drags into February and one fumbles with numb fingers at the ordinary knots and hooks of life. People are irritable, difficult. Some days you want to stay in bed with the covers over your head and dream of paradise. A place where the warm sea washes the white sand. There are a few palm trees on the higher ground, many brightly colored fish in the lagoon, waves breaking on the reef farther out. No one in sight. Occasionally an incredibly large, split-second shark darkens the clear water. Sea birds ride the wind currents, albatross, kittiwake ... and pass on. Day after day, sea wind and perfect sky ... You make a big heap of driftwood on the beach.

JANUARY

Daytime highs are well below zero. The air is absolutely clear and dry, the wind sharp, precise. We walk about in our bulky clothes like spacemen or old-fashioned divers on the bottom of the sea. The snow crunches underfoot. Now, above a single bare birch tree in the middle of a field of untrodden snow, the evening star appears in a most extraordinary blue sky. Everything is hard-edged, clear-cut. A perfect world made of glass. The sky is the exact color of Mary Beth Anderson's eyes. Beautiful, perfect. Perfect hair and perfect teeth. It always seemed that she knew exactly what she wanted and where she was going, that she had planned her life in detail. One thing I know for sure, she would have had no time for anyone who dresses the way we do.

INDECISION

People died or moved away and did not return. Things broke and were not replaced. At one time he had owned a car and a telephone. No more. And yet somehow, things did not become more simple. Then one night, roused from sleep he stepped out naked into the below zero winter night, into the clear midnight and twenty billion stars. Nothing stirred, not a leaf, nothing out there, not the animal self, not the bird-brained self. Not a breath of wind yet somehow the door slammed shut locking behind him and knocking the kerosene lantern to the floor. Suddenly the whole place was afire. What to do? Should he try to make the mile-long run through the woods over hard-crusted snow to the nearest neighbor or just stick close to his own fire and hope that someone would see the light? The cabin was going fast. Flames leaped high above the bare trees.

THE WAY THINGS USED TO BE

When we moved out here thirty years ago there weren't so many paved roads. There were fewer houses, fewer people. There weren't so many lights. Could be there's more of everything now. It seems to me we get more snow now than we used to. We were a long way from town in those days but we didn't see so many animals. There were tracks, only suggestions ... I'm sure we see more moose nowadays. It was quiet. There was the wind in the spruce trees that seemed sometimes as if it were saying something, but wasn't. Often on clear nights you'd see the aurora. Basically, though, there was nothing out here. That's changed. It's hard to explain the way things used to be. It's hard to find words to explain the loss of nothing.

FEBRUARY

for Michael Van Walleghen

Snow falls upon snow. It piles up on the roads, mile after gray mile of it catches in the wheel wells of the car. It piles up like debt, like failure, and, as your mother pointed out, you've put on a few pounds since Christmas. Now in February the winter seems permanent, glacial. Each snowfall is more a feeling than an external event, a heaviness, shortness of breath. You wake in a panic, tearing at the blankets. It's only a cat. A large house cat. You've wakened in an overheated room in a strange house with the family cat sleeping on your chest. You are a guest, you don't belong here. Heart pounding, you want to be on your way. But it's the middle of the night, in winter. There's no place to go. You won't be here very long. Relax. Nothing has changed. You are who you've always been, only more so.

ROAD SALT

A big orange truck comes along spreading sand and salt on the icy road. Sand, salt, freshly ground pepper ... with a few minutes cooking the road is ready, done to a turn. You can be on your way. But salt is not content just to eat the snow and ice. It starts in on your automobile. Rust spots develop, then holes where the salt has eaten through. Though you wash the car scrupulously salt finds secret, hidden spots and eventually the floor falls, dumping the passengers and their luggage in the road. Eventually the whole car collapses into a heap of rusty powder and scale. A white, salty residue gathers on your shoes as you walk away. You could repair those rust spots now, before the worst happens, but life is short. Who has time for that?

SNOW PEOPLE

Being mostly water as we are, it's not so bad living in a cold climate like this one. It gives you a certain solidity. Cold feet, the icy handshake, the cold shoulder, the frozen countenance, shouldn't be thought of as ill will but as a kind of preservation. When life touches life more heat is given off than is ordinarily healthy. Just look at the way my ears have begun to droop from the things whispered there. There are fires without and fires within. It won't do any good to throw yourself into the fire, you can't become the flames. In every case those who do end up as a small puddle of water that someone else steps over at the end of winter.

MARCH

It hadn't occurred to me until someone at work brought it to my attention that this winter has been going on for eleven years. I said, "That can't be. Surely not." But then I got thinking about it. It was eleven years ago November we moved into this house. You remember, snow was just beginning and we had so much trouble getting the refrigerator down the driveway and through the door. Danny was eight and we got him a sled for Christmas. It's amazing how one gets concerned with other things and the time just goes by. Here it is March and now that I've noticed it, the snow has begun to melt a little. During the day there's water running in the street. It's like a bird singing in a tree that flies just as you become aware of it. When you think about it, the world, cold and hard as it is, begins to fall apart.

The Winter Road

2000

STORY

The things that happen willy-nilly in life, lawsuit, gum disease, romance ... must be given, if not meaning, at least some context. Each has to be incorporated immediately into the story you tell yourself. And the sooner the better. In order to avoid unpleasant surprises, things should be written in before they occur. But now I've gotten ahead of myself. There I am, my future self, my shadow stretching out thirty feet ahead on the winter road: enormous feet, wide legs, big fat ass and a torso tapering away to a tiny, pin head. This is not a true likeness, of course, the distortion caused by my distance from the sun. But it gives you the idea. The truth, the absolute truth, is like absolute zero, more a hypothesis than an actuality. If you could experience it you wouldn't like it. It's cold enough as it is. The truth is an imaginary point, like the vanishing point. It's as if there were a point to this story. As if when you got to the end you could remember what happened in the beginning.

THE TELEPHONE

In the old days telephones were made of rhinoceros tusk and were big and heavy enough to be used to fight off an intruder. The telephone had a special place in the front hallway, a shrine built into the wall, a nicho previously occupied by the blessed virgin, and when the phone rang it was serious business. "Hello." "One if by land and two if by sea." "What?" "Unto you a child is born." "What?" "What did he say?" "Something about the Chalmers' barn." The voice was carried by a single strand of bare wire running from coast to coast, wrapped around a Coke bottle stuck on a tree branch, dipping low over the swamp, it was the party line, all your neighbors in a row, out one ear and in another. "We have a bad connection, I'm having trouble understanding you."

Nowadays telephones are made recycled plastic bags and have multiplied to the point where they have become a major nuisance. The phone might ring at you from anywhere, the car, the bathroom, under the couch cushions ... Everyone hates the telephone. No one uses the telephone anymore so telephones, out of habit or boredom or loneliness perhaps, call one another. "Please leave a message at the tone." "I'm sorry, this is a courtesy call. We'll call back at a more convenient time. There is no message."

TUMBLING TUMBLEWEEDS

Out on the Great Plains, where I was born, the wind blows constantly. When I was a kid I'd get 35 cents and run as hard as I could to the Lotta-Burger or the movie theatre only to find it had blown away. Going home was no better. Sometimes it would take a couple of days to find my house. Under these conditions it was impossible to get acquainted with the neighbors. It was a shock to open the front door and be faced with the county jail, the Pentecostal Church, or Aunt Erma carrying two large suitcases. Trash from all over the state caught and piled up at the edge of town, and during the windiest times of spring sometimes whole days blew away in a cloud of dust. I feel my natural lifespan may have been shortened by the experience. Still, it was a great place to grow up. As the old boy said, "You can have those big cities, people all jammed together. Give me some wide open spaces." In the morning out on the plains you have a couple of cups of coffee, get all wound up and go like hell across an open field, try to bounce, clear both ditches and the highway so you don't get caught in the barbed wire, fly from one fenced-in nothing to another, hit the ground and keep on rolling.

CORONADO

Coronado came up from Mexico in search of a life of the imagination. The Zunis said, "Oh God, here comes Coronado and those Spaniards." The Zunis drew a line on the ground with cornmeal and said, "OK Coronado, cross that line and you'll be sorry." But of course he crossed. The Zunis said, "Seven Cities of Gold? Go see the Pueblos." So on he went, but the great cities did not appear, only mud houses. The Pueblos said, "Oh yeah, the Seven Cities of Gold, they're over northeast, way over, maybe five hundred or a thousand miles." So he set out again. There was nothing, day after day, no gold, no silver, not even an ATM, just the wind blowing through the prairie grass. Coronado was a determined man who knew that hard work and patience would be rewarded. But when he got to Kansas he realized that this had to be a joke or else that someone had been badly misinformed.

MUDHOLE

Life has no meaning. Right at the center of anything you can name there's a big nothing, a hole large enough to drive a truck through. But nobody dies just because of that. My grandfather farmed for years around a mudhole right in the middle of his already meager acreage. A kind of curving ditch known as "the creek" though it seldom held any water. The mark of the harrow and the mark of the plow followed the contour of the bank making a pleasing pattern in the dirt. The way the lines of a poem are pleasing (something about seagulls, the sun going down and the dust behind the tractor, rising in a tall column, so that it was visible even from the County Line Bar two miles away) or like bars of music, which has no meaning either. Someone can take a perfectly good drinking song, turn it into an anthem, people enlist, and things get a whole lot worse. But meanwhile, back at the tavern, the music goes on and so does the drinking.

SUNFLOWERS

The few we managed to twist off their tough, sap-sticky stalks Mother would not allow inside. So we put them in an empty fruit jar on the back porch where they slumped over forgotten and died. They grew everywhere, in the ditches, around the barns, the bright yellow and brown whizzing past you in the car on the Saturday drive into town like spots before your eyes. What fun! Sprawling into the untended fields, over the abandoned farms, jumping up and down in the back until the seat springs broke.

A MIRACLE

When my father was eight he cut his foot on a broken bottle hidden in the tall grass and got blood poisoning. Inexorably the red line rose toward the heart and the doctors could do nothing. Then one evening just at dark the gypsy healer came to the door. No one had called her, an old woman with many layers of odd clothes, long skirts, scarves and a man's raincoat. She examined the foot, muttered some words, a prayer perhaps, and said "Here. The poison is here." She made a swift cut with a small knife that seemed to appear suddenly in her hand. "You must soak the foot in very hot water and Epsom salts for one hour, three times a day. In three days the child will be well." And it worked. The healer stopped by each day around sunset to examine the wound. Strangely, she would take no pay. She went back to the gypsy camp, to the horses and wagons, the dark-skinned men in white shirts, the ragged children. One morning, a week later, my grandfather woke to find that all the chickens were gone, every single one, only some feathers on the floor of the silent coop. The gypsies were gone too, vanished in the night. Miracles always have a cost. When one thing is repaired another breaks. When something is healed, something else dies. So the old woman took nothing, knowing God would provide.

THE PREACHER

When times were hard, no work on the railroad, no work down on the farm, some of my ancestors took to preaching. It was not so much what was said as the way in which it was said. "The horn shall sound and the dog will bark and though you be on the highest mountain or down in the deepest valley when the darkness comes then you will lie down, and as the day follows the night you will surely rise again. The Lord our God hath made both heaven and earth. Oh, my dear brothers and sisters we know so well the ways of this world, think then what heaven must be like." It required a certain presence, a certain authority. The preacher was treated with respect and kept at a bit of a distance, like a rattler. There wasn't much money in it but it was good for maybe a dozen eggs or a chicken dinner now and then.

A HILL OF BEANS

As children we were given inaccurate information. Things turned out to be much different than we were led to believe. Adults were not entirely to blame for this because most of them had no more idea what was going on than we did and found themselves bewildered at every turn, baffled by the impossible complexities of life. So instead of real insight we were given aphorisms. Gems such as, "life is no bed of roses" or "you can lead a horse to water but you can't make him drink." Of course, society has changed radically, even in my lifetime. Therefore the rather agrarian quality of these sayings has caused them to lose some of their original impact. "You aren't going to amount to a hill of beans." Which, to me, suggests laziness, shiftlessness, failure, poverty, rambling discourse, idle speculation ... I suspect that "a hill of beans" refers to the fact that beans are of little value even in large quantities and also that they make very poor hills. Yet, I can't help imagining a really important hill, a great Bunker Hill of beans, or a San Juan Hill of slippery pork and beans up which a frustrated Teddy Roosevelt is trying to charge.

CRIPPLE CREEK

Five of us crammed into my car. I drove. I think it was my idea. I'd read something and I had a map. For some reason I thought I knew what I was doing. And nobody objected! It seems amazing to me now, how willing they were to risk their lives, careening around the mountain backroads. I think we made it. We survived. Where were we going? Was there someone I was longing to see? I don't remember. It was important. But no matter how much I think about it, there is no destination. Just the little green car flying around the switchbacks, rocks, pines, the clear sky, the wheels throwing gravel into the air and over the edge.

HIGH FINANCE

"It takes money to make money," my father said, "you have to have something to invest." We all nodded and made affirmative, muttering sounds. "Take care of the nickels and the dollars will take care of themselves," my mother said. "Some people are born with a talent for making money," my father said, "but you've got to have a start, a little bit of luck." "Thrift. Thrift and hard work," Mother said, "that's what my parents taught me." We all stared silently into our coffee cups. "Owning your own business," Father said, as if he hadn't heard Mother at all, "that's the way to make money. You'll never make any money working for someone else." "Nonsense," Mother said. "That's all pie in the sky." "Pie in the sky," we thought, "mmm ... pie in the sky!" Pie with great cumulus mounds of ice cream, served on silver platters, inside those castles in the air. Pie in the sky ... cloudberry pie.

CIMARRON

"Cimarron roll on
to my lonely song."
Sons of the Pioneers

Except for periodic floods the river didn't so much roll as kind of amble. "A mile wide and a foot deep," they said. In dry times the sandy riverbottom was like a beach, a shore with no ocean. But the water was moving, leaving behind the bloated carcass of a hog rotting in the sun, carp and catfish trapped in rapidly evaporating pools, a whole steam engine sunk beneath the quicksand, a house collapsed where the bank eroded away. The river wandered away as in a dream, no explanations, no parting words, the door ajar, newspapers blown across the floor, dirty dishes left in the sink. . . .

RADIO

When I was a kid I listened to the radio late at night. I tuned it low as I could and put my ear right up next to it because my dad didn't like it. He'd say, "Turn off that radio. It's after midnight!" No matter how low I tuned it he could still hear, from down the hall and through two closed doors. He was tired. It had been a long day, his muscles ached but still he was nervous, on edge and this was just one more thing, the final thing, keeping him from the sleep, the absolute dead silence he wanted. As for me, whatever music I was listening to, some rock station way down on the border, probably, (100,000 watts of pure power!) has become even more faint over the years. But I can still hear it.

Two

WIND IN THE TREES

You could live on the go like the wind with what seems like a purpose or at least a direction, but no home, reckless, pushy, with an attention deficit disorder, no more than a name, really. People will say, "That guy, you know …" But if you stand still long enough you will be given an identity. You could live like the trees, parochial, rooted and restless, prone to hysteria. You could write letters to the editor. Living in the woods you get a lot of ideas about what God is up to, and what is going on in Washington. You'd have a family. Parents, grandparents, aunts and uncles all close around you until, if you are lucky, they recede, one by one, into the peripheral haze of memory. Finally, some space, a clearing, a place to fall.

PILGRIMAGES

People come from hundreds of miles away to walk along this shore. They like it especially when the sea is violent and flings itself against the rocks. The solitary pilgrim walks head down, hands in pockets, collar turned up against the wind, muttering, "I know what you mean, I know just what you mean." Then he goes away. As he must, as we all must. Even if you sleep every night at the door of the temple, in shadow of the shrine and sell maps of the Holy City, the time will come to go on pilgrimage. Suppose, for thirty years, you've been holding a downspout to a stone wall. It's not a job you intended to keep for so long, but time slips away. Then one day you're offered a new position, suspending a muffler and tailpipe, trying to maintain the integrity of a Chrysler product. Somewhere the restless heart must be satisfied. So away you go, in a cloud of smoke, and the long, winding road turns out to be short. And straight as a dog's throat.

YOUR SHIP

Officials of the Kalends Ship Line today denied having any knowledge, "at this time," of the *Danaïd* or its cargo and were unavailable for further comment. Nevertheless your ship is out there somewhere, sailing under a flag of convenience, bound for either Marseille or Jakarta, rolling on the oily swells, the cargo shifting slightly with each rise and fall.

Last night during middle watch the mate caught sight of a woman below deck. He recognized her immediately as the woman he'd seen in the hotel lounge the night before they sailed. Long hair and heels, the jacket of her suit slung over her shoulder, she was whistling a little tune as she turned and disappeared down a dimly lighted passageway.

APPARITION

She said, "Take me to California. I want to see the ocean." As soon as I said yes I knew it was trouble. Right away I could see myself on the streets of Los Angeles without my wallet or maybe even without my pants. As it turned out I got no farther than Utah before I found myself hallooing into culvert openings. Now I've got myself into this and can't see a graceful way out ... The next morning bright as a penny, another sunny honeymoon on the dusty road, all on my own with the grasshoppers and the rattlesnakes, still a hundred miles from anywhere. She was beautiful and said all the silly things I wanted to hear. She said, "Come with me and you can have your own life."

JAZZ POEM

I always wanted to write one of those Jazz poems. You know the kind, where it's three a.m. in some incredibly smoky, out of the way, little club in Chicago or New York, April 14, 1954 (it's always good to give the date) and there are only a few sleepy people left in the place, vacant tables with half-empty glasses, overturned chairs ... and then Bird or Leroy or someone plays this incredible solo and it's like, it's like ... well, you just should have been there. The poet was there and you understand from the poem that jazz is hip, intellectual, cool, but also earthy and soulful, as the poet must be, as well, because he really digs this stuff. Unfortunately, I grew up listening to rock and roll and decidedly unhip country music and it just doesn't work to say you should have been in Gary Hofstadter's rec room, July 24, 1961, sipping a Pepsi, listening to Duane Eddy's latest album and playing air guitar.

BAD PLACE

The story is that the Dacotah would never make their camp here, that the horses would bolt whenever they came near. It's a bad place and nothing can be done about it. No amount of urban renewal will help. The brick crumbles and the boards rot. There is broken glass under the streetlight and nightshade grows in the alley. It's a low place where the air is bad, a kind of depression located halfway up and halfway down. This place is the very center of a Bermuda triangle that's bounded by Thanksgiving, Christmas and New Year's. Uncle Karl is drunk and Aunt Liz is crying... This is the place that, every day, no matter which route you take, you have to walk through on your way home.

MAY

Finally, no amount
of kindness or
generosity will help.
In May the song sparrow
returns. Hidden
in the spring green
his only gift is his song,
all the sweeter because
it isn't meant for you.

THE PROSE POEM

The prose poem is not a real poem, of course. One of the major differences is that the prose poet is incapable, either too lazy or too stupid, of breaking the poem into lines. But all writing, even the prose poem, involves a certain amount of skill, just the way throwing a wad of paper, say, into a wastebasket at a distance of twenty feet, requires a certain skill, a skill that, though it may improve hand-eye coordination, does not lead necessarily to an ability to play basketball. Still, it takes practice and thus gives one a way to pass the time, chucking one paper after another at the basket, while the teacher drones on about the poetry of Tennyson.

AS THE LIGHT TURNS GREEN

The faith of saints is absolute. There is order beyond all this dying, eating and begetting. Beyond the work week there is reason that, in the fullness of time, will be made manifest. A saint is lifted as a solitary star into the firmament. One by one, as the light turns green, we mortals merge into the Great Flow but a saint will cross six lanes of traffic to reach the posited exit.

FLORIDA

This morning at the university I passed a young woman in the hall who was wearing a very tight orange t-shirt with FLORIDA printed on the front in large white letters. Naturally I thought of citrus fruit. I thought of orange groves with workers tending the smudge pots on cold nights. I thought of Wallace Stevens in his white suit, walking barefoot on the beach, carrying his shoes with the socks tucked inside, and I imagined the moon over Miami. I have never been to Florida but I know there are drug dealers, red tide, walking catfish, Republicans, Disney World, alligators, hanging chads ... Still, the citrus fruit is very good this time of year and when I peel an orange and look out the window at the snow and the rough spruce trees it seems like a miracle. One taste and I know there is a world beyond my imagining. It's impossible, like love, yet it really exists.

AQUI

People say things you can't understand, the air is strange and the pale, daytime moon is in the wrong position. So far from home all that you assumed becomes stretched to a thread, more narrow than the highway through the Sierra de Guanajuato, stretched so thin, in fact, that for fear that it might break, one is careful, while lying in the shade of the bougainvillea, not to make any sudden moves. Now, in the Plaza de Nuestra Senora De La Luz, in the midafternoon heat, almost nothing moves. The burro, loaded, as ever, with fifty-kilo sacks, is tied to the jacaranda tree, where he has always been, where he always will be. He twitches an ear when a fly lands on it—but not when the bells of the Oratorio begin their clamor.

CEREMONY

One day you cross an invisible line and everything is changed. But what? It is as if you had crossed the international dateline, all at once it's another day. Now everything you looked forward to is suddenly behind. What did you hope for anyway? And why? Neither love nor money will help. Your previous life is hearsay and is inadmissible as evidence. Perhaps, during the night while you slept, there was a ceremony to mark the occasion, a party. Books and papers are scattered everywhere and, obviously, someone has stolen your reading glasses. Hijinks. Perhaps King Neptune himself, in his iron crown, presided over the court as you were ushered into a new world. It's morning. The ship sails on, same as ever, into the blue.

RIVER GORGE

I could carve out
a little place for myself
in 10,000 years or so,
but long before that life
would have gone all strange
and none of the landmarks
would be familiar.
Like the water
I'm just passing through,
only I'm not taking
anything with me.

PICNIC ON THE SHORE

Shore grass growing among the big rocks enduring year
after year. This is the way to live. A simple life, the proper
arrangement of a few elements. But here you are standing
on slippery stone, trying to balance a full plate and a cup.
What with the wrappers, the flies and the wind, already
things have gotten out of hand.

Three

DULUTH

"A baby, eh?" That's all he says. She never says he's the father but they get married anyway. This way the city gains another citizen. But for each one that's born another dies or moves away and things remain pretty much the same. The mayor has been dead for several years but we think he does a better job that way and we keep him in office. Once in a while Bob Dylan comes back to town, but he never calls. We prefer it quiet, understated. At one o'clock Sunday morning the snow plow passes with its flashing blue light and then, ten minutes later, a car, silent, muffled by the snow. A light still shines in the attic apartment of a large house two blocks over. These old houses, once the mansions of mining millionaires and lumber barons, are full of secrets. Some properties have been completely restored and in others people keep bears as pets. If you are outside around dawn you might catch a glimpse of someone taking the bear for a walk and think "Why would anyone want a big dog like that? But then ..." you say to yourself, "there are all these new people in town."

CHANGE

All those things that have gone from your life, moon boots, TV trays and the Soviet Union, that seem to have vanished, are really only changed, dinosaurs did not disappear from the earth but evolved into birds and crock pots became bread makers and then the bread makers all went to rummage sales along with the exercise bikes. Everything changes. It seems at times (only for a moment) that your wife, the woman you love, might actually be your first wife in another form. It's a thought not to be pursued ... Nothing is the same as it used to be. Except you, of course, you haven't changed ... well, slowed down a bit, perhaps. It's more difficult nowadays to deal with the speed of change, disturbing to suddenly find yourself brushing your teeth with what appears to be a flashlight. But essentially you are the same as ever, constant in your instability.

IRON

Iron is purely masculine, containing perhaps too many Y chromosomes. Iron lacks the flexibility and strength of steel which is tempered by the feminine element. Iron lacks delicacy, but does not lack courage. Iron is hard work and sweat. Iron is passion without finesse. A long time ago a man discovered that he could make an impressive sound by dragging a large piece of iron through a field of stones. Iron is divorce, child-support payments, poorly-planned crime, dishes in the sink, wool socks drying over the coal stove. Out back there's the hulk of a '57 Chevy still awaiting restoration. What glowed red hot in youth is cold as a pump handle in middle-age.

NORTHERN LIGHT

Matisse and Monet had plenty of light. They were pro-
fligate, slopping Mediterranean sun everywhere. Vermeer
had to buy it, a little at a time, import it from Africa or
someplace. It ruined him, finally, the costly gold leaf and
the precious ultramarine. In the north the light has to be
concentrated and focused. Each detail must be accounted
for, placed carefully just this side of darkness. Here a bit of
sun on a yellow building and here light from the window,
illuminating her face and highlighting the folds of her
dress, the map on the wall, the letter in her hand. News
from far away, we imagine. We can't know if it's good
news or bad, but then, any word the light brings is better
than no word at all.

FIRE DANGER

When conditions are right, it takes only the smallest spark to set the entire forest on fire. Like love, kindled by the merest glance or a smile, even though the two of you have nothing at all in common. It's the chance arrangement of positive and negative ions. You say, "We have so much in common, so much more than Elaine and I ever had." You say, "Sometimes we talk for hours. We have so much to talk about." All summer, all through September and October the winds stirred in the dry timber. Now in November, the leaves are down, and the cold rain falls day after day. "So what?" you say to yourself, "So what?" You tell your friends, "It's wonderful. I've never felt like this before. I'm so unhappy." And your friends run away when they see you coming.

LATE OCTOBER ABOVE LAKE SUPERIOR

A north wind shakes the last few yellow leaves clinging to a thin popple tree. It's easy to tell what's coming. Old leaves must fall to make way for the new. That's all well and good as long as it's not your turn to go. Keep the dead waiting! Keep the unborn waiting! There's not much to this life anyway, some notions, some longings that come and go like the sea, like sun and shadow played across the stone. This weather is not so bad if you can find a place among the rocks, in the sun, out of the wind.

HEAVEN

Heaven is a state of such perfection that it is difficult to describe. It lacks the irregularities of life that make a good story, that make people realize they are alive. But, of course, in heaven people aren't alive. There is little to say of the day-to-day as there are no days or nights. So conversations begin "Back when I was alive ..." or "When I lived in Chicago ..." In my dream we were riding in a car, we were in back. I fell asleep and dreamed that you touched my hair, while I slept. It was a dream within a dream, an infinity of mirrors, reflecting nothing, finally. When I woke from one or another of my dreams I found a hairpin in my hair that must have been one of yours. In heaven I will carry it in my pocket. That is, if in heaven we have pockets.

PIONEER FARM

Think of spending the winter alone here, in this two-room cabin. Think of spending it here with someone else. The settlers were frugal. They used newspaper for toilet tissue, newspaper for chinking between the logs, the words carefully mouthed and puzzled over then shoved into a crack. Once a month someone made the long trip into town to sell the eggs and buy a newspaper. They used feedbags for dresses, harness leather for door hinges, snot for bubble gum. The Bible was their only book. Mother was crazy and Father was a tyrant. The eldest daughter ran off with a sewing machine salesman. The first son ran away and set up his own little monarchy, just like this one. Everyone is gone now, even the owl who used to roost in the barn. It's not a good place for a farm, the growing season too short, the ground too rocky. What I hate most is the lingering sanctimonious air, the condescending forgiveness.

MAILBOXES

Some are brightly painted and large as if anticipating great packages. Most are smaller, gray and dented with rust spots; some held together with rope or duct tape, having been slapped more than once by the snow plow. Still they seem hopeful ... perhaps a Village Shopper or a credit card offer ... Once in awhile one raises a modest tin flag. "I have something. It isn't much. I'd like you to take it." All along Highway 2, on Hunter Road and Dahl Road, past Cane Lake, past the gravel pit, and the last refrigerator shot full of holes and dumped into the swamp, mailboxes reach out on extended arms, all the way to the end of the route where balsam and spruce crowd together in the ditches, reaching out. . . .

THE LOON

A loon surfaces suddenly not more than ten feet from the boat. How rare to be so close to this wild and beautiful bird! An unexpected joy. But quick as thought he vanishes, slips silently under water again. The loon is neither memory nor desire nor anything you imagined. If you are observant you will notice that the loon does not regard your sudden appearance as particularly beneficial. And when he surfaces again, far behind your back, he is not laughing, though it seems so.

SUNDAY MORNING

I remember Sunday mornings in church when I was a child, then dinner at Aunt Pearl's house. The endless afternoon in the backyard with only her arthritic Pekinese for company, while inside the adults talked on and on about people who were dead. Think of learning the multiplication tables, true love, and the hours spent sitting on the edge of the bed in shorts and a t-shirt biting fingernails. I learned to smoke and to drive a car, how to cook spaghetti. Maybe all of that counts for something, and maybe someone, somewhere has been keeping score. Something like Social Security. Maybe one day I'll be given some sort of compensation (with certain deductions and penalties, no doubt) for accumulated life experience. Enough, perhaps, for a double-wide modular home on some rather low ground in an outlying district of what may not be heaven, but could certainly be a lot worse.

HOCKEY

Ice hockey makes very little sense to the innocent bystander. Yet people in this area are passionate about the sport, so, like religion and politics, it is a subject best not brought up in polite conversation. The players, with their skates and heavily padded uniforms (which for some strange reason include shorts) all trying to whack the puck into one or the other of the nets, seems, to the uninitiated viewer, a very approximate operation, something like trying to knit while wearing boxing gloves. One of the biggest problems for the spectator and, evidently, for the players as well, is that the puck is hard to see. It is so small and shoots across the ice at great speed or gets caught beneath a mass of fallen players. This causes a great deal of frustration among the players, which they vent upon one another. Long ago, before we became so politically correct, hockey was played using a recently detached human head as a puck. More brutal perhaps, but much easier to follow the puck.

OUR NEW HOUSE

Our new house is too small to hold a real ghost or even a poltergeist. It is more a cottage than a house, nevertheless there are things that go bump in the night, enough to wake you from a sound sleep. We are not yet quite settled in and our possessions have not all decided on a place. One morning I found my toothbrush on top of the refrigerator and today apparently, the geranium prefers to suffer next to the window. Everything seems to desire change. A young woman marries, against her parents' wishes, a man from New Jersey of doubtful reputation. In subsequent generations the family knack for mathematics is lost, as is the talent for horsemanship. What remains is a characteristic willfulness. And the prominent nose. Everything wants to move. Even the flour canister musters just enough sleepy energy to fall from the shelf to the floor, spilling its contents. Yet it maintains a slightly ridiculous attitude of dignity even in abject defeat.

ROCK COLLECTING

On Hegberg Road I found a really big agate, big as my fist, half buried in the dirt. I dug it out using a sharp rock as a digging tool. It took nearly fifteen minutes to dislodge the stone from the roadbed. I washed off the dirt in the ditch water and on closer examination I discovered that it wasn't an agate after all, just an ordinary reddish-colored rock, jasper maybe. What a relief! I could drop the rock back in the road. I could go on with my life.

Four

BACK HOME

The place I lived as a child, the sharecropper's farmhouse with its wind-bent mulberry trees and rusted farm machinery has completely vanished. Now there's nothing but plowed fields for miles in any direction. When I asked around in town no one remembered the family. No way to verify my story. In fact, there's no evidence that any of what I remember actually happened, or that the people I knew ever existed. There was my uncle Axel, for instance, who spent most of his life moving from one job to another, trying to "find himself." He should have saved himself the trouble. I moved away from there a long time ago, when I was a young man, and came to the cold spruce forests of the north. The place I thought I was going is imaginary, yet I have lived here most of my life.

PAINTING AND WRITING

I have a letter written by my great-great grandfather in 1902, full of the moment: "There are several cases of smallpox reported in Frederick." Yet despite the distance, the changes, there is an immediacy in the language. "Sim (a son-in-law) has sold $600 worth of wheat. He's thinking of buying a new buggy. I'm helping him paint his barn." It takes forever to paint one of those big barns. I think if I could find the place—somewhere southwest of Lyons— they'd still be at work, Sim on the high wooden ladder painting traditional barn red and the old man on the ground, painting the white trim around the doors and windows. So much work going into a structure that will fall down in fifty years, or less. It's awkward, difficult for any of us to know what to say. The past and the future are the same, finally. A time where you aren't. And you do what you do because it's the thing that you do.

"Well, this has certainly been interesting. Now, whose boy are you again ...? Well, anyhow I'd better get back to work this barn won't wait."

"No. You can't let your brush dry out."

"Yes, use it or lose it, as they say. Ha, ha. Say hello to everyone ..."

THUNDERSTORM WARNING

The National Weather Service has issued a severe thunderstorm warning effective until two a.m. Viewers should expect heavy rain, hail, damaging winds, dizziness, nausea, headache, fainting, disorientation, uncertainty, loss of direction and the questioning of deeply held beliefs. Persons in the warning area should seek shelter immediately. If you are caught out in the open you should lie face down in a ditch or a depression.

BERRY PICKING

This time of year, mid-summer, we drive out the Matson road to pick thoughtberries, so called because once you spend a day picking you will think twice about ever doing it again. Thoughtberries don't grow in the deep woods but in the marginal, burned-over ground, in the scrub and scrap, in those awful swampy, bug-infested thickets out where the blackflies eat you alive. Thoughtberries are not plentiful. Sometimes it takes an hour of hard labor, picking the low stickery bushes to gather just a handful. Their scarcity must be the most of their appeal because, really, they aren't all that good. Small, tough and sour, they need a lot of sugar to make them palatable. There are not enough of them in these parts to make them a commercially viable product, but then in many parts of the country they don't grow at all.

A BEAR AND HIS MONEY

Every fall before he goes to sleep a bear will put away five or six hundred dollars. Money he got from garbage cans, mostly. People throw away thousands of dollars every day, and around here a lot of it goes to bears. But what good is money to a bear? I mean, how many places are there that a bear can spend it? First you have to locate the bear's den, in fall after the leaves are down. Back on one of the old logging roads you'll find a tall pine or spruce covered with scratch marks, the bear runes, which translate to something like "Keep out. That means you!" You can rest assured that the bear and his money are nearby, in a cave or in a space dug out under some big tree roots. Though sometimes the young males just flop down on the ground. You have to be careful. When you return in winter, a long hike on snowshoes, the bear will be sound asleep ... In a month or two he'll wake, groggy, out of sorts, ready to bite something, ready to rip something to shreds ... but by then you'll be long gone, back in town, spending like a drunken sailor.

HEY DIDDLE DIDDLE

I like the high times as much as anyone, the music and the jokes. I like the night, the wine, the shadows of trees on the path, the secret places on the periphery of the light, the breeze soughing in the tall pines. I can stay awake until ten o'clock, even eleven on weekends. Still, these days I'm happy when everything glides to a landing on the soft grass, when the guests have gone. I like the sound of the door closing, the latch catching, the light clicked off. But now it is nearly two in the morning and here I am lying awake. My dish is still out there somewhere, in the mad moonlight, last seen in the company of a spoon.

BLUE, BLUE DAY

Some days are so sad nothing will help, when love has gone, when the sunshine and clear sky only tease and mock you. Those days you feel like running away, going where no one knows your name. Like slinging the old Gibson over your shoulder and traveling the narrow road to the North where the gray sky fits your mood and the cold wind blows a different kind of trouble. Nothing up there but mosquito-infested swamp, 10,000 acres of hummocky muck, a thicket of alder and dogwood, a twisted tangle of complications where not even Hemingway would fish. But somebody, someday soon, somebody will come and put up a bed and breakfast and a gourmet coffee shop. There is only one true wilderness left to explore, those vast empty spaces in your head.

THREE DOGS

THE DOG OF THE DEAD

Sometimes I wake in the middle of the night and all is quiet except for a dog barking. A flat, repetitive barking that has the rhythmic qualities of someone driving a nail into a board. This is his job, the graveyard shift, to which he brings no enthusiasm but only a dogged persistence. He must be the dog of the dead since his owners never respond to his alarm.

IMAGINARY DOG

A man stands in the path holding a dog leash calling into woods, "Here Maggie. Here Maggie." When I approach he says, "Don't worry about my dog, she's awfully big but really gentle. She sometimes likes to jump up and lick people but she's never bitten anyone, well, there was the postman that time but he surprised her and it was really only a nip ... Here Maggie. Here Maggie." I smile and pass by. There is no sign of a dog, only dense forest on either side of the path.

BLACK DOG

I don't own a dog and I don't want one, but every now and then a black dog accompanies me on my walk out on Winter Road, which is strange because there are no houses nearby, yet he seems well fed and content. He usually approaches from behind silently and walks alongside me. The first time he appeared it caused me to jump, but I've grown to expect him. As company he is only a little better than my own thoughts, ranging ahead or lagging behind to sniff at something in the ditch. We walk along, each without acknowledging the other, and when we part at the end of my hike neither of us says good-bye.

OLD MAN WINTER

Old man Winter doesn't like anything. He doesn't like dogs or cats or squirrels or birds (especially seagulls), or children or smart-ass college students. He doesn't like loggers or environmentalists or snowmobilers or skiers in their stupid spandex outfits. He doesn't like Christmas or television, or newspapers for that matter. He doesn't like lawyers or politicians. There is a thing or two he could say to the host of the local talk-radio show but he knows for a fact that the son-of-a-bitch does the broadcast from his condo in Florida. He's pissed off about the OPEC oil conspiracy and the conspiracy of gas station owners to raise prices. He can't stand the current administration and didn't much like the last one, either. He doesn't like foreigners and he doesn't like his neighbors (not that he has many); and when they finally die they just leave their junk all over the yard. He doesn't like that. He doesn't like the look of the sky right now, either, overcast, a kind of jaundice color. He hates that. And that stand of spruce trees behind the house turning black in the dusk … The way it gets dark earlier every day. He doesn't like that.

CONJURER

After years of practice you are able to produce the illusion of a human figure: a man, perhaps. A man wearing a navy blue suit, a middle-aged, more-or-less law-abiding citizen. The finer points, however, still elude you. For one thing, you've gotten the ears too large, the hair is unruly, unkempt looking and the sleeves of his jacket and the legs of his pants are too long, or else his arms and legs are too short. The brown shoes are on the wrong feet. No matter how you try the figure isn't quite right. On the other hand, fog and trees are fairly easy to conjure up and help to mask the errors. The droplets of water weighing down the delicate needles of the tall pines gives the scene a sort of oriental look, a kind of ancient dignity. And it gives the figure a rather contemplative aspect, the monk alone in the wilderness. But now the suit looks out of place ... Passersby will say, "Did you see that goofy looking guy over there in the trees?" "Goofy, yes... but very well dressed."

JACKSTRAW

You look for deeper meanings in things. There are signs and portents, though sometimes you deny it. You find special significance in certain places and days, the cottage by the lake, Christmas, a certain Chinese restaurant in Winnipeg, your birthday, and set them up like signposts marking the passage of your life. One after another they multiply until you're surrounded by a forest of sticks. Jackstraws. Touch one and they all fall down. Jack Straw, head full of hay, reading long boring books, waiting for the mail, watching the days go by. Here it is Sunday morning and there's no one downtown but the looney and dysfunctional. There's old One-Eye who recently returned from Jupiter, and the spooky Woman in White, Tom Drooley, Mr. Ozone Peepot, Euclid and The Motorcycle Queen, Mr. Occupant, Goofy Walker, Old Man Winter, still wearing his down parka. It's spring. It's April Fools. It's the Easter parade! Grab your hat and let's get in line!

SOMERSAULT

Some children did handsprings or cartwheels. Those of us who were less athletically gifted did what we called somersaults, really a kind of forward roll. Head down in the summer grass, a push with the feet, then the world flipped upside-down and around. Your feet, which had been behind you, now stretched out in front. It was fun and we did it, laughing, again and again. Yet, as fun as it was, most of us, at some point, quit doing somersaults. But only recently, someone at Evening Rest (Managed Care for Seniors) discovered the potential value of somersaults as physical and emotional therapy for the aged, a recapturing of youth, perhaps. Every afternoon, weather permitting, the old people, despite their feeble protests, are led or wheeled onto the lawn, where each is personally and individually aided in the heels-over-head tumble into darkness. When the wind is right you can hear, even at this distance, the crying of those who have fallen and are unable to rise.

FLIGHT

Past mishaps might be attributed to an incomplete understanding of the laws of aerodynamics or perhaps to an even more basic failure of imagination, but were to be expected. Remember, this is solo flight unencumbered by bicycle parts, aluminum and nylon or even wax and feathers. A tour de force, really. There's a lot of running and flapping involved and as you get older and heavier, a lot more huffing and puffing. But on a bright day like today with a strong headwind blowing up from the sea, when, having slipped the surly bonds of common sense and knowing she is watching, waiting in breathless anticipation, you send yourself hurtling down the long, green slope to the cliffs, who knows? You might just make it.

THE NAME

Instead of an idea a name comes to you, a name that no longer has any connection to the owner of the name. It comes as sound merely, rhythmic, musical, exotic and foreign to your ears, a sound full of distance and mystery. A name such as Desmond Tutu, Patrice Lamumba or Kofi Annan. You forget the names of acquaintances and the name of your first true love but this name comes to you. It repeats like a tune in your head. It refuses to go away, becomes a kind of mental mumbling. You say it to yourself over and over. This is your mantra, "Boutros Boutros Ghali …" Then suddenly as it came, the name vanishes.

Deep in the night, long after your own name has flown away, a voice wakes you from a sound sleep, a voice clear and certain as the voice that summoned Elijah, saying "Oksana Baiul."

Sea Smoke

2004

IMAGINARY READER

If poetry is your life, then your life must be the poem, a life that exists only for the reader. And who is the reader for whom you write? The imaginary reader? Perhaps it's a beautiful woman who is so taken with the words that she reads late into the night, propped on one elbow, only a sheet covers the curve of her hip, slipping away from her bare shoulder. The summer breeze from the window teases her dark hair. Her lips move, from time to time, ever so slightly as she repeats a phrase that seems especially moving ... But probably, the imaginary reader is even more vaguely described, like God. The reader reads. Nothing happens. Nothing changes. The night goes on. He is still reading. He yawns, rubs his eyes. Any moment now the book will slip from his hands, so you write faster.

THE BODY AND THE SOUL

Long ago I was told that the body was the temple of the soul, a temporal dwelling for the eternal soul. I suppose the body could be thought of as a dwelling, it has plumbing and electricity, it groans and creaks in the night. I think in most cases, however, it's more like a modest bungalow than a temple. And the house idea does not accommodate human mobility. Perhaps a motor-home would be a better analogy. The body is the motor-home of the soul where the soul sits behind the wheel and drives the body here and there, back and forth to work, off to the seashore or the Rocky Mountains. But the soul is a bad driver, so often distracted, dwelling on higher things, pondering, moving slowly up the pass, traffic backed up behind for miles. The soul gazes idly out the windows (eyes) paying no attention whatsoever to the road, and is in danger of sending the entire metaphor plunging over the precipice.

BLUE MOON

The moon looks worried, rising above the lake. The moon looks so unhappy, so pale. The moon has not been well. The moon has had a lot of problems with meteors, especially in youth. And night after night, the same earth rises ... It hasn't been easy for the moon. The moon ... The moon ... The moon this and the moon that. You drive faster but the moon keeps pace, looking sadly into your car window. "Why are you leaving," the moon wonders, "and where will you go?"

THE TALK

He liked her immediately, her blue eyes, the way she listened, as if what he said was fascinating, the easy, natural way she laughed at all his jokes. Her rather conventional good looks and dress belied her intelligence. They had things in common, an interest in art and humanism. She talked about the problems of coffee growers in Central America. He listened but he also thought about kissing her on the neck, where her blond hair curled just behind her ear. He thought about other things, too. Mostly they laughed. Then she was silent. She looked at him. He saw that her eyes were gray, not blue. She was serious. She said, "Matt, this has gone too far in too short a time. I feel as though I'm being smothered. I have no time to myself anymore. I feel like you are always there. And I can't even so much as speak to another man …" "What are you talking about?" he said, "We only met an hour ago!" "That is exactly what I'm trying to say," she said.

CULINARY CONSIDERATIONS

Lyle can't eat any onions or garlic. Phil is allergic to shellfish. Steve has a violent reaction to celery. Patricia is allergic to beef. Connie cannot eat processed meat. No fat for Joe. Dennis cannot eat any spicy food. Frank believes he is allergic to vinegar. Georganne is unable to tolerate mayonnaise. Michael is allergic to eggs and certain fish. Charlie and Sue do not eat meat, except fish. Thomas will eat no vegetables and no fish ... "Ick!" Dylan eats no meat or dairy products, except once when he ate an entire large cheese pizza. Peter will not eat cheese. Richard won't eat anything. Almost no one drinks anymore except Walt who drinks too much and has to be sent home in a taxi. Elaine cannot stand Caroline so they have to be seated at opposite ends of the table.

THE KISS

When I was eleven or twelve years old I thought a lot about kissing girls. Since I had never kissed a girl, romantically, that is, I was unsure how to go about it. I tried to imagine grabbing a girl roughly, as sometimes happened in movies, turning her around and kissing her hard on the lips. ("She struggled a moment then succumbed to the power of his passionate kiss ...") Betsy O'Reilly would have knocked me down. How much pressure did one apply, should the lips just touch, lightly? (And what about French kissing? I could not imagine ...) What was the proper duration of a kiss? The movies of that day often ended with a long kiss, the couple embraced, the music rose, but then the image faded. After the kiss what happens? Do you just stand there sort of embarrassed, shuffling your feet? You'd have to say something, but what? "Thank you for the really swell kiss, Alexandra?" The logistics were formidable. I thought about kissing a lot but I began to see that it was impossible.

THE FIRST DAY OF SPRING

When one is young, every day (as I remember it) is the first day of spring, all headlong and heedless. But, it turns out that life really is short and before you know it you are old and filled with sadness. Nothing to do now but watch the birds, scratch a few petroglyphs for someone to puzzle over years from now, stay out of the way and leave the bulk of the wanton destruction to those who are younger. The human race will evolve or go extinct. So what? It happens all the time. You never see saber-toothed tigers anymore. I suppose I should be sorry about that, but to tell the truth I never liked them. All that screaming and prowling around outside the house at night——who needs it?

FISHERMAN: STONEY POINT

Here's an old guy talking to himself. He reels in his bait and says, "Son, you've got to go out there again. I know the rocks are treacherous, the water is deep. The winds can come up suddenly and there's no more than the thinnest line ties you to me. This is the way your life is going to be, out and back, again and again, partly in this world, partly in the other, never at home in either. Still, it's what you were born to do. You are young and strong, all steel and hooks. You know I'll do everything I can to bring you back safely. Go out there boy, and bring home a big fish for your old father to eat."

A HAPPY SONG

We know that birds' singing has to do with territory and breeding rights. Male birds sing to attract females and warn away other males. These songs include threat and intimidation, and perhaps, in the more complicated songs, the insinuation of legal action. It's the grim business of earning a living in a grim world. Each song has its own subtle sound, the idiosyncrasies of its singer. It turns out, though, that the females don't really value innovation and invention and generally mate with males that sing the most ordinary, traditional tune. There is always though, some poor sap that doesn't get it, sitting alone on his branch practicing and polishing his peculiar version until it flows smoothly as water through the streambed, a happy song that fills us with joy on this first warm day of the year.

THE BACK COUNTRY

When you are in town, wearing some kind of uniform is helpful, policeman, priest, etc. Driving a tank is very impressive, or a car with official lettering on the side. If that isn't to your taste, you could join the revolution, wear an armband, carry a homemade flag tied to a broom handle, or a placard bearing an incendiary slogan. At the very least you should wear a suit and carry a briefcase and a cell phone, or wear a team jacket and a baseball cap and carry a cell phone. If you go into the woods, the back country, someplace past all human habitation, it is a good idea to wear orange and carry a rifle, or, depending on the season, carry a fishing pole, or a camera with a big lens. Otherwise, it might appear that you have no idea what you are doing, that you are merely wandering the earth, no particular reason for being here, no particular place to go.

HEREDITY

I have come to recognize certain genetic traits that I have inherited, patterns of behavior, certain involuntary actions. I can feel them happening, that worried look of my mother's, that almost angry, I-deserve-better-than-this look. And my father's manner of clearing his throat, the sleeves of his work shirt rolled to the elbow, a pencil poised motionless above a scrap of paper lying on the yellow oilcloth that covers the table, next to the white porcelain salt and pepper shakers with the red metal tops. Which means it must be sometime in the 1940s. The war still going on. Neither of them saying a word, as if stunned there in the dim late-night light of the kitchen. And what am I doing here? I should have been in bed hours ago.

WHERE GO THE BOATS

Green leaves a-floating
Castles of the foam,
Boats of mine a-boating—
Where will all come home?

        R. L. Stevenson

Legend has it that the great Chinese poet Li Po made his newly composed poems into paper boats and let them float away down the Yang Tze. I recommend this practice to poets of today, particularly beginning poets, as an alternative to submitting poems to literary magazines. I do this chiefly because I believe that the chances of your poem actually being read are greater using this method.

If you send poems to a literary magazine the unopened envelope goes, along with hundreds of others, into a large cardboard box in one corner of an office. Then once every six months or so, someone, a volunteer from a rehab program perhaps, comes, opens the envelopes, throws the poems into the trash, places printed rejection slips in the return envelopes, seals the envelopes and takes them all to the post office. If you send poems to the most "important" literary magazines the unopened submission goes immediately to the paper shredder.

But suppose, by some mischance, some failure of the system, your poem is published. It won't be read. Just the words "literary magazine" are enough to send a chill to the heart of the most voracious reader. Copies of the magazine will, after having their covers ripped off, be thrown onto a back shelf of a used bookstore, which smells of mildew.

How much more noble to think of your poem plying the waters of the Susquehanna or the Verdigris or the Mississippi. Think of your poem being pulled ashore by an astonished reader in Davenport or Baton Rouge. Or imagine your little poem boat sailing at last into the open sea, bravely alone.

CANARIES

I remember when I was a child, I had a pair of canaries in a cage in my bedroom. I had the idea that I would raise and sell canaries. I asked one of my sisters if she remembered them. She remembered that they were parakeets, not canaries. I asked another sister. She said she didn't remember any canaries, but she remembered how mean I was to her. My youngest sister doesn't remember having birds, but thinks that we had a pet rabbit. I don't remember that. My brother thinks we had a pet crow that talked. I don't remember a crow but I remember we had a myna bird for a while that said, "How ya doin'?" but he belonged to someone else. My mother says that she would never have allowed birds in the house. I remember how the female canary ignored the male, but chirped plaintively to a mockingbird that sang outside my window all summer long.

THE CANADIAN WILDERNESS

I was awakened during the night by something inside my sleeping bag rubbing against my back near my shoulder blade, scratching me. I reached around and it felt like one of those stiff cloth labels, the kind they attach to pillows and mattresses and such, the ones that say DO NOT REMOVE UNDER PENALTY OF LAW. I grabbed hold and gave it a yank, and much to my shock, found that it was attached to my back! I lay there a few moments, my mind racing, my back still in pain where I'd pulled at the label. I tried to calm down. I must have been dreaming. I felt again, carefully. It was definitely attached to my back. I didn't know what to do. Should I wake the others, say, "I've got a mattress label attached to my back!" What could they do, anyway? It isn't really a medical emergency and we're camped deep in the Canadian wilderness, no phones, no roads, a hundred miles from the nearest settlement. Outside the sky is clear, a nearly full moon shining over the lake, no sound except for a little breeze in the spruce trees. It's beautiful. Nowhere to go, nothing to be done.

OVERBOARD

A piece of folded paper comes flying down from the deck above, over the stern of the ferryboat, and I have the split-second shock of something irretrievably lost. Well, it isn't a child overboard. It isn't even the Magna Carta, pitched into the deep. Perhaps it's an old love letter, written in a loopy hand with little hearts dotting the i's, thrown ceremoniously by someone at the end of a marriage or an affair. Maybe it is a suicide note, tossed by someone who has reconsidered. Maybe it's the plans for a failed invention, or the first page of a bad novel. Most likely there's just some dope up above dumping garbage, a shopping list, or nothing, a blank piece of paper. It is just something that happened, anything, made memorable only by circumstance. The paper lingers there in the flat water at the center of the boat's wake and then, before you know it, is ten years past, a tiny speck. And then it's gone.

THE CLOUDS

The clouds sweep toward the western horizon as if they were nomads. Horses, men, children, dogs, and wives, cookpots and knives, feathers, flags, ribbons, and hides, skulls borne on tall poles, all caught up in the whirl, the ecstasy of motion. They set off with a will, as if inspired. It is as if they served the great Kahn himself, a man of such presence that simply to behold his majesty would remove any doubt. To hear him speak banishes all hesitation. It is their manifest destiny! "Onward!" They would follow him across continents, across oceans if necessary... But the thoughtless clouds move only at the behest of the wind, who is no one at all.

BASSOON

The very slightest of winds moves the curtains, the violins faint tremolo just before dawn. Then you hear again the voice you know so well, a voice at once your own and not your own, a voice that may have gone on all night long and, for all you know, may continue long after your eyes have closed. The sound of a bassoon, perhaps, that wanders vaguely as a bumblebee from flower to brick wall to water bucket, yet is clear and sweet in the early light before the full cacophony of the day begins. Birdsong. Children's voices. Flutes and piccolos, quick, high-pitched and somewhat annoying. "Oh, Grandpa," they say, "not another one of your long, boring stories!"

FREE LAWN MOWER

There's a broken down lawn mower at the curbside with a sign saying FREE. And so I ask myself, what does freedom mean to a lawn mower? A lawn mower that has only one job and no outside interests, a job which it can no longer perform? Gone the days of the engines roar, the cloud of blue smoke, the open lawn, the waves of cut grass left in its wake, the flying gravel, the mutilated paper cup. Freedom could only mean the freedom to rust away into powder and scale. Most likely the lawn mower will be thrown into the back of a beat-up truck by a guy who sees its potential as scrap, a guy who will seize upon anything of even the slightest value, anything free.

POPPLES

In places where there are fewer trees, people call them aspen and they are highly prized. Up here they are known as popples, scrap wood. Not very good for lumber or firewood, but good enough for paper, and the armyworms love them. They grow everywhere. Wherever there's an opening, the popples move in, any abandoned clearing, any yard left untended. Popples are excitable, quivering all over at the slightest hint of a breeze, full of stupid chatter, gossip, rumor and innuendo. The proletarian popple tree, growing, optimistic, got the kids all working, grandkids on the way ...

Popples are lovely in fall when the leaves turn yellow and gold, or in winter with a new moon caught in the branches, and in spring when the rain enhances the delicate grey-green color of the bark. I wouldn't mind a view like this when I come to the bottom of the slide into old age and senility: a stand of popples judiciously framed by the bedroom window to exclude the junk car and the trash cans just to the right.

SURVEYING

One of the first jobs I had was surveyor's helper. There were three or four of us in a crew; we worked all over Oklahoma and west Texas, surveying lines for power lines or gas pipelines. In brushy country this could be a slow process, since trees and other obstacles had to be cleared from the line of sight. The best surveying was in the high plains of west Texas. Here the transit man could see for miles. Two of us walked, measured the distance and drove stakes. The last member of the party was the engineer, the boss, who wrote down figures in a little book. Most of what we'd do would be to mark a straight line across the country, from point A to point B, making calculated turns only when absolutely necessary. All very precise, in theory. It was a good job. We got to travel, eat in greasy cafes and sleep in dumpy motels. In the evening we drank beer and teased the girls in the bar. Best of all I was young and free. Here were the endless plains, the vast cloudless sky. I could walk across Texas forever. As long as it was in a straight line.

THE WEDDING

"Where is the wedding? What time does it start?" "I don't know. What did you do with the invitation? What shall I wear?" Someone said it was at St. Paul's then someone else said that at the last minute the couple decided to fly to Las Vegas and get married at a drive-up chapel. Never mind. It's the ideal wedding, the ideal couple.

Turns out we've missed the ceremony. As we arrive the minister is walking away from the church carrying his robes over his arm. It was hotter than usual today. He is smiling slightly as he walks, thinking of the newlyweds, thinking of a gin and tonic.

The old folks have gathered on the church lawn to chat. Summer hats, white shoes, pink dresses, powder blue sport coats. "Who was the bride?" No one is sure. The grand daughter of a friend? A distant cousin's niece? "But wasn't the bride beautiful?" "And the groom, so handsome— well, everyone says he's smart, has a very important job."

Meanwhile the bride and groom have gone to the rose garden to be photographed. Clouds are gathering in the west. Thunderstorms are predicted. It makes us unreasonably happy to see the bride and groom in their silly outfits, smiling at the camera—the air full of threat and promise, the smell of rain and of roses.

SLEEPING BEAUTY

Everything outside had changed, the faces, the styles, the landscape was altered, even the language had changed, making the people difficult for the nobility to understand. At first the outsiders had been curious and those inside the castle had a kind of celebrity status. But the novelty wore off. In the new world there was no need for these ancients. The prince and his crew ran everything and though the prince loved the princess, there was no getting around it; the age difference was a factor in their relationship, she being exactly 100 years older than the prince. At times she found his immaturity trying. He spent so much time away from the castle in the company of knights he brought from his father's kingdom, involved in politics or real estate deals. She was left alone with her parents and the others who still suffered the residual effects of the curse. The castle became more and more isolated, as if the briars had grown up again to surround the walls and those inside sleepwalked from room to room.

JULY

Temperature in the upper seventies, a bit of a breeze. Great cumulus clouds pass slowly through the summer sky like parade floats. And the slender grasses gather round you, pressing forward, with exaggerated deference, whispering, eager to catch a glimpse. It's your party after all. And it couldn't be more perfect. Yet there's a nagging thought: you don't really deserve all this attention, and that come October, there will be a price to pay.

I SAW MAMA KISSING SANTA CLAUS

What neither junior nor his father knows is that she sees him every time he phones. The off-season, mostly. So it isn't true that Santa only comes once a year. She does her hair, her makeup, and puts on the little black dress he likes so much, and her heels. She goes to meet him in some little out-of-the-way joint downtown. It's difficult for a high-profile guy like Santa to be discreet. What does she see in him anyway? Overweight and god knows how old, red-faced, slack-jawed and snoring now in room 308 of the Seafarer's Hotel? Well, it's true, he can be fun, his humor and generosity are legendary. But she sees this can't last. Perhaps though, despite her slight feeling of disappointment and the obvious impossibility of the whole affair, she still holds out some faint hope. A belief in something wondrous about to happen, that somehow this year will be better than last.

A SENSE OF DIRECTION

I hope no one reads anything I've written with the expectation of finding any meaning or direction. I have no sense of direction whatsoever. Yet occasionally, as I walk along in my private fog, someone will stop and (probably saying to himself "Here's a guy who's obviously been around here for a hundred years") ask how to get from wherever we are to, say, the Mariner Mall or the Club Saratoga. So I oblige this person with detailed instructions accompanied by elaborate gestures, pointing, and maps drawn in the air. We part mutually gratified, each feeling a sense of accomplishment. Later I realize that my account had fatal flaws, and I imagine the lost soul saying, "What an idiot!" or "What a liar."

Nevertheless, there are a lot of books out there, and a few of them actually contain accurate information. But these books all have the same limitation: they were written for the living. One is only alive for a short while and dead for a very long time. Yet, as far as I know, no one has written anything that's of any use to the dead.

RETIREMENT

I've been thinking of retiring, of selling the poetry business and enjoying my twilight years. It's a prose poem business, so it's a niche market. Still, after thirty-six years, I must have assets worth well in excess of $500. Perhaps the new owner of the business will want to diversify, go into novels or theatre, maybe even movies or perhaps merge into a school or a movement. It won't matter to me once I've retired. Maybe I'll do a little traveling, winter in the Southwest. Take up golf. Spend more time with the family. Maybe I'll just walk around and look at things with absolutely no compulsion to say anything at all about them.

AUTUMN LEAVES

"And you call yourself a poet!" she said, laughing, walking toward me. It was a woman I recognized, though I couldn't remember her name. "Here you are on the most beautiful day of autumn ... You should be writing a poem." "It's a difficult subject to write about, the fall," I said. "Nevertheless," she said, "I saw you drinking in the day, the pristine blue sky, the warm sunshine, the brilliant leaves of the maples and birches rustled slightly by the cool west wind which is the harbinger of winter. I saw how you watched that maple leaf fall. I saw how you picked it up and noted the flame color, touched here and there with bits of gold and green and tiny black spots. I'm sure that you saw in that leaf all the glory and pathos, the joy and heartache of life on earth and yet you never touched pen to paper." "Actually," I said, "most of what I write is simply made up, not real at all." "So...?" she said.

HALDEMAN & ERHLICHMAN

Very few people remember Haldeman & Erhlichman, and even fewer know which is which. Which goes to show that even infamy is fleeting. "Haldeman & Erhlichman ..." people say, "Haldeman & Erhlichman. One of them is dead. I'm sure of that. Maybe both of them are dead." Haldeman & Erhlichman, one of the lesser known of those comedy teams that include Burns and Allen, Abbott and Costello, Hamilton and Burr. Haldeman & Erhlichman still play Republican fundraisers in places like Keokuk or Kokomo. They appear at Henry Kissinger's annual birthday party. They sing, they do magic tricks. "Hi! I'm Haldeman!" "I'm Erhlichman! One of us has a crew cut." "Can you guess which one?"

MIDDLE AGES

We have come now to the middle ages, our own private Middle Ages. It is a time of poverty and ignorance, the king's knights trampling the fields, destroying the crops, the peasant's hovel on fire, the pigs loose in the cabbage patch. And from behind the monastery walls, comes the sound of mournful singing. It is an age of faith, I suppose ... So, what comes next? It seems to me that we must be going backwards. We long ago passed the Age of Enlightenment. It must be the Dark Ages yet to come. Already rooks have gathered in the oak tree and the long ships have hoisted their black sails to set forth on stormy seas that are the color of your eyes.

AWAKENING

When I open my eyes it appears that I'm still here, same hands, same feet, same room, you still here beside me as you have been, thankfully, for years, and the early light coming in the window as it always has. But appearances, as we know, can be deceiving. I'm putting on my white tie, baby, put your blue dress on! Let's go out there and see how many people we can fool.

APPLE DOLLS

To look at their faces you'd think they remembered childhoods of summer, long hours at the old swimmin' hole, hayrides, blueberry pie, the county fair, kisses stolen under a sky full of stars. You'd think those wrinkles came from many years of hard work, sun and wind: the men in the fields, the women cooking, washing clothes, raising a dozen kids. But as they were born old, in their clean overalls and gingham dresses, they are perfect rubes, literally born yesterday. They don't even remember last week's bingo game or Tuesday's "Meals on Wheels" lunch, and indeed, that may be the reason for all this rosy-cheeked merriment.

THE ASH GROVE

The black ash is the last tree to grow leaves in the spring and the first to lose them in the fall. Broken limbs, ragged bark all patchy with lichen, they scrape by in the swamp where not much else will grow. Most of the year it's difficult to say if they are dead or alive. And today with a low overcast sky and a cold wind blowing they look even more forlorn. So, I have a lot of sympathy for the black ash tree.

I walk out here to clear my head, which really isn't necessary because there really isn't much going on in there. Most of what I'm told goes in one ear and out the other. I stop and listen. Nothing but wind in the trees. Oh, but what if I forget everything? What if I forget how to tie my shoelaces or blow my nose? And the forest all around heaves a great sigh.

DINER

The time has come to say goodbye, our plates empty except for our greasy napkins. Comrades, you on my left, balding, middle-aged guy with a ponytail, and you, Lefty, there on my right, with the pack of cigarettes rolled up in your t-shirt sleeve, though we barely spoke I feel our kinship. You were steadfast in passing the ketchup, the salt and pepper, no man could ask for better companions. Lunch is over, the cheeseburgers and fries, the Denver sandwich, the counter nearly empty. Now we must go our separate ways. Not a fond embrace, but perhaps a hearty handshake. No? Well then, farewell. It is unlikely I'll pass this way again. Unlikely we will all meet again on this earth, to sit together beneath the neon and fluorescent calmly sipping our coffee, like the sages sipping their tea beneath the willow, sitting quietly, saying nothing.

FICTIONAL CHARACTER

They called me into an office, told me how much they liked my work, appreciated my loyalty, etc. In the end they handed me a pistol, showed me how to shoot it and told me that I had to get rid of Edgar because Edgar was a danger to the organization, perhaps even a threat to national security. What organization? I thought this was an advertising agency. The problem is that I have a lousy author, a ham-handed hack. He goes for action and suspense: cheap tricks. Besides that, I rather like Edgar. He is described as "handsome, athletic, good natured, not given to introspection." Then there's Holly, beautiful Holly. We've just started going out together, things are going well between us, and it could lead to a "deeper relationship." Why would I want to ruin that? Any author will tell you that, finally, he has no control over his characters. Once created they have a will of their own and go their own way. So I told them I would have to think about it. I took the pistol and locked it in my desk drawer. I wondered if I should call the police. The thing I had not anticipated was what happened when I introduced Edgar to Holly.

OLD COUPLE

They walk hand-in-hand through the park. They must be well into their eighties and probably neither remembers exactly how they got together in the first place. It was so long ago. They are almost the same height and nearly the same shape in their matching sweaters and walking shorts. They walk very slowly. It looks as though either, or both, could fall over any minute. They hold hands the way they did when they first met, for hours, until their palms became sweaty. Both afraid that if they loosened the grip, the moment would be lost, that their happiness would somehow vanish. Now they hold hands to steady one another in a world that seems so terribly changed. This is a kind of tug-of-war as well. Which will tire first, lose interest, and let go?

HITCHHIKER

I pick up bull thistles and burdock, beggar ticks, cockle-burs, sandburs, seeds of all sorts, on my pants legs as I walk the fields and ditches. Somewhere, way down the road, some will fall on fertile ground and begin the haphazard garden all over again. I pick up pebbles in my shoe treads and when they fall out they spawn streambeds, glacial eskers, mountain ranges. One day there will be a huge boulder right where your house is now, but it will take awhile.

KNIFE ISLAND

From Stoney Point it appears as a green, rounded shape in Superior's waters, perhaps a safe haven, the Promised Land, like the Lake Isle of Innisfree rising from the mist. Up close it's just a pile of rocks with a few stunted trees, a place beaten by water and wind; a squalor of seagulls. The whole place is covered with gulls, gull shit, feathers and broken eggs, gulls in the air, gulls on the water, gulls on the ground. It's a noisy place, threat and intimidation, outrage, and indignation, the constant squabbling over territory. They cry, "justice!" "You are in my space!" Seagulls, like humans, not comfortable alone, not happy together. This is life with all its horrible enthusiasm, better seen from a distance.

STEADY OR SLOWLY FALLING

Around this time every year the gloom swallows up someone unexpectedly, at random, it seems. We try to find reasons. He was depressed. He ate too much sugar. It seems hopeless, trying to figure things out. And yet, someone figured out the lever and the inclined plane. Someone invented glue and sandpaper and someone learned which mushrooms were good to eat. Thank god it wasn't all left to you, you can't even boil water. But there's no use whining that your parents didn't leave you proper instructions or adequate tools, you simply have to make do. A stick to dig roots and grubs for the soup, and you have learned, by now, that it takes only a light tap with the same stick to put the baby down for his nap. Now, with the snow falling outside, the soup bubbling in the pot, the baby sleeping soundly in his crib, there's time for a moment of reflection ... Then the phone rings, and the baby starts crying just as the pot on the stove boils over, and, between one thing and another, your feet get tangled in the phone line. Which is a length of string tied to a couple of tin cans.

PARK

You could think of it as a small park. Well, not exactly a park, a little space between two busy streets, a city beautification project, an afterthought of city planners, all nicely bricked, with a park bench and an old maple tree that predates any planning, nothing else. It's a space nobody uses, really. Nobody sits on the bench. The drunks throw empty wine bottles here, now and then. And occasionally a bird, a crow or a sparrow, lands on a bare branch of the tree, on its way elsewhere. You could think of the leaves that have fallen as all of your dreams and hopes that have fallen and blown away, now that it is November. But there is no park really, and no bare branch where a bird could land. There is only this empty space that you cherish and protect, where once your heart was.

TIME MARCHES ON

How quickly the days are passing. "Time passes," people say. As if time were a kidney stone, as if it were a freight train or a parade. Crazy Days, Wrong Days in Wright, Rutabaga Days, Duck Days, Red Flannel Days. Gone the Black Fly Festival, the Eelpout Festival, Finn Fest, the Carnivore's Ball, the Five-Mile-Long Rummage Sale; all have passed. What has passed is forever lost. Modern Dance on the Bridge Abutment, The Hardanger Fiddle Association of America Meeting, the Polka Mass, "O, lost and by the wind grieved ..." The Inline Skate Marathon, the Jet Ski Grand Prix ... What is past is as though it never was. The Battle of the Bands, the Polar Bear Plunge, the Monster Truck Challenge, the Poetry Slam ... But you came specifically to see the "Barbie Doll Drill Team, Drum and Bugle Corp." And perhaps that's them coming now ... No, it's the Nashwauk-Keewatin High School Marching Band. It's a long parade. You shiver a bit in the chilly east wind. It's getting late and it occurs to you that you may never get back to work.

IV

SUBLIMATION

In scientific terms, sublimation is the direct conversion, under certain pressure and temperature conditions, of a solid into a gas, bypassing the liquid state. That's why that patch of ice on the sidewalk gets a little smaller every day even though the temperature never gets above zero. Something similar happens whenever I deposit a check into my bank account. The funds never reach a liquid state. It's the same when, thirty years later, you visit the house you lived in as a child. It's much smaller than you remember. People are older and smaller. Everyone notices when something dramatic happens—a car crash, a tree falling over. Yet the subtle process of the sublime goes on continually, without much notice. Whatever was continues to be, in the form of molecules or atoms or something, no more available now than it was back then.

THE LONG WINTER

The winter here is so long that one needs to find an outdoor activity to pass the time. Some people ski or snowboard. There's snowmobiling, ice skating, hockey ... I prefer ice fishing. Standing around in the cold wind all day, pulling ice fish from a hole in the ice. Ice fish have to be eaten raw, like sushi. If you cook an ice fish you wind up with nothing but a skillet full of water. Gnash one down or swallow it whole, there is nothing like the flavor, full of the glittering, bitter cold of a January day. Your teeth crack, your tongue goes numb, your lips turn blue and your eyes roll back in your head. "God!" you say, "God that was good! Let me have just one more."

AN ILL WIND: PARK POINT

Today there's a cold northeast wind blowing, Ice has piled up all along the water's edge like piles of broken glass giving off a strange blue light. Park Point is deserted, no one for five miles down the beach. Just the way I like it. The sand is frozen, mostly, so the walking is easy as I pick my way through the wrack and drift. Today I don't even leave footprints. Wind, sand, sun and water, a simplicity that defies comprehension, the barest essentials for the imagination's work. This shore has been pretty much the same for ten thousand years. Countless others have been here before me, musing and pondering, as they walked down the beach and disappeared forever. So here's what I'm thinking: wouldn't it be great if one of them dropped a big roll of hundred dollar bills and I found it?

I MUST SAY

Now that we have come so far together, so much water gone under the bridge, and now that the shadows lengthen around us, I feel that I must say some things that are difficult for me to say ... This is a world of plague bearing prairie dogs and freshly fried flesh. Where is the fish sauce shop, and when did the Irish wristwatch shop shut? Are our oars oak? Are the sheep asleep in the shed? I cannot give you specific statistics but surely the sun will shine soon. Surely the sun will shine on the stop signs and on the twin-screw steel cruisers.

I have lain awake nights thinking of how to say this. I can only hope that what these words lack in meaning will be somehow compensated for by your understanding of my need to say them, and by your knowing that these words are meant for you. Though who you are in this context is never made clear, and it is quite possible that you, yourself, do not know.

THE BLACK JOURNAL

In the black journal there are a number of entries about the weather and the slant of the winter light. There is an observation of how sea smoke rises from the cooling body of water, along with some unintelligible scribbling about form and substance. On page 21 there are a few ideas for financial reorganization. Then on page 23 some notes about ice fishing. After that there are many, many blank pages.

DARK DAYS

Overcast skies, the threat of snow, the day is a lingering twilight that makes these big white pines seem even more ominous. At any moment one of these old trees could fall, killing me instantly. Here's what the investigating officer told the newspapers: "It was an act of God, pure and simple. Some people don't believe in God's existence but something like this just goes to prove it." Which causes me to wonder, was it predestined or just a moment of extreme annoyance? The forest gives rise to such gloomy speculations. We stand around, no real answers, not much to say, and nothing to do until another wind comes along, sending us into a fury of pointless activity.

LOST

It's remarkable, the honesty people exhibit in regard to lost mittens, particularly, a single mitten, and really that is all you ever see. The finder picks up the mitten and places it in a prominent place, on a tree branch or a window ledge, where it can be easily spotted by the searcher. Days go by, but the owner of the mitten does not return. A mitten lost is gone forever, separated from its mate for eternity. It's always that way it seems. One mitten, one shoe on the freeway, one nearly new sock alone in the drawer, having never really gotten to know its missing partner. But here at Lover's Overlook, there's a pair of panties, a splash of bright red in the weeds. One imagines mayhem or, possibly, wild celebration. But no one expects the owner to retrieve the lost item.

GOINGS ON AROUND THE HOUSE

There's a spider crawling up the wall towards the crown molding and I don't like the looks of him. I know you can learn by watching spiders. I know about Robert the Bruce and Whitman's noiseless, patient spider. But maybe Whitman's hearing wasn't all that good, maybe that spider was going about his work whistling, a kind of annoying, tuneless whistle. Whitman said he could go and live with the animals, and people do. Generally, though, we tend to be rather choosy about which animals. People often want a certain breed of animal, a Jack Russell terrier or a Siamese cat, nothing else will do. Of course, there are people who live with rats and snakes, and god knows what else. I don't care. There is a spider on my ceiling and I don't like him.

OLD FRIENDS

There's a game we play, not a game exactly, a sort of call and response. It's one of the pleasures of living for a long time in a fairly small place. "You know, they lived over by Plett's Grocery." "Where that bank is now?" "That's right." "Plett's, I'd almost forgotten. Do you remember where Ward's was?" "Didn't they tear it down to build the Holiday Mall?" "Yes." "I remember. The Holiday Mall." It works for people, too. "Remember the guy who came to all the art exhibit openings, the guy with the hat?" "Yeah, he came for the free food and drinks?" "Right." "And there was the guy with the pipe and the tweed jacket who always said hello to everyone because he wasn't sure who he actually knew." "Oh, yes!" It's like singing an old song, *la, la, la,* and you actually remember some of the words. And when you have gone someone will say, "Oh him. I thought he was still around. I used to see him often, only, all this time, I thought he was someone else."

THE STATE OF THE ECONOMY

There might be some change on top of the dresser at the back, and there are some pennies in a jar in the closet. We should check the washer and the dryer. Check under the floor mats of the car. The couch cushions. I have some books and CDs I could sell, and there are a couple of big bags of aluminum cans in the basement. Only trouble is that there isn't enough gas in the car to get around the block. And the price of gasoline goes up every day. I'm expecting a check sometime next week, which, if we are careful, will get us through to payday. In the meantime with your one-dollar rebate check and a few coins we have enough to walk to the store and buy a quart of milk and a newspaper. On second thought, forget the newspaper.

REMEMBER

I'm trying to take up less space. I'm trying to remember to pick up after myself, to remember to take off my muddy boots before I come into the house. It's difficult. Partly because one branch of my family can trace their lineage directly back to an extinct species of water buffalo. I have to learn to talk quietly. To eat slowly, keeping my mouth closed. To wash and dry my little bowl and spoon and put them away. Turn off the lights, close the door softly. Descend the stairs carefully, avoiding the step that creaks, so as not to wake the dead that are sleeping shoulder to shoulder. Those so long dead that their names and dates have eroded from their tombstones. The dead that can turn over in their narrow graves without ever touching the body next to them.

OF AN AGE

I'm getting to an age when, if I suddenly dropped dead, most people would not be overly surprised. And, no doubt, there are some who would welcome the news. I'm not particularly looking forward to it—death and whatever comes after. Which is not much by the look of it, decomposition and discorporation, when all the microorganisms that makeup this conglomerate go their separate ways, thus ending one instance of corporate greed and mismanagement. But possibly some will linger, talk of an employee buyout, some wearing buttons that say "Solidarity Forever." Most likely, there will be a few farewell parties with drinks and reminiscing, balloons, a joke sign saying, "Will the last to leave please turn out the lights?"

SOME THINGS TO THINK ABOUT

How cold is it? Will you need to wear your long johns or will the heavy wool pants over your blue jeans be enough? Which socks? Which boots? Which jacket? Scarf? Do you need the choppers with wool liners or just gloves? How fast will you be moving? If you are skiing or, God forbid, going to the mall, will you be too warm? Which direction is the wind from? Is it better to walk into the wind on your way out and have it at your back on the return, or vise-versa? Do you have a choice? Will the car start? Do you have blankets, fire extinguisher, flares, window scraper, extra gasoline, gas-line antifreeze, starting fluid, lock deicer, windshield washer fluid, a shovel, fresh water, flashlight, matches, candy bars? Do you have enough Kleenex? Ask yourself what you have forgotten. Do not ask yourself why or how. Remember to take your car keys out of your pocket before you put on your gloves.

THE CHAIR

The chair has four legs but is a whole lot slower moving than, for instance, the ostrich, which has only two. Sometimes the chair does not move for weeks, even months at a time. Despite this sedentary almost catatonic lifestyle it could be argued that the chair is every bit as intelligent as the ostrich, whose brain is smaller than its eye. And the chair is far less dangerous and unpredictable than the ostrich. The chair is more thoroughly domesticated. But it isn't a lazy boy, don't slouch, don't lean back too far or the chair will throw you, for sure. The chair invites you to relax but to remain upright and attentive. The chair invites you to come to the table, sit down and eat your big bowl of ostrich stew.

WAYFARING STRANGER

There are places in the world that, because of time and money or inclination, I am never going to visit: Iquitos, for instance, or Archangel, the Ross Ice Shelf, Baltimore. There are places in the woods just outside town where I will probably never go. There may be a square foot or two of swampland out there where no human being has ever stepped, or at least, not for a long time. There is an outside chance I might wind up there one day. There are parts of my own back yard where I hardly ever go, especially in winter when the ground is covered with snow. And then, even when spring beckons, I often decline the invitation. Inside any house there are remote and seldom visited corners. Suppose you found yourself behind a closet door, or in the dusty attic, in the damp recesses of the basement, in the company of spiders and sow bugs. You might come to yourself slightly exhilarated, but uneasy, a bit heartsick so far away from home.

THE SNOWMAN MONOLOGUES

I don't have the top hat like my ancestors—well, my predecessors—had. I've got a mad bomber hat. Quite trendy, I think. I've had to give up the pipe and I never drink. Still, I've got a big smile for everyone. I'm a traditionalist. I like the old songs, "White Christmas," "Ain't Misbehavin'," "Don't Get Around Much Anymore," songs like that. But I try to stay up to date, I'm very concerned about global warming, for instance, but it's difficult in my field to get any real information. And what can I do? Not that I'm complaining. I feel at home here, very much a part of my environment. It does get lonely at times though, there are so very few women in these parts and I'm not the best looking guy around, with my strange build and very odd nose. Sometimes I think they put my nose in the wrong place. Still, I have always hoped that someone would come along, someone who would melt in my arms. A woman with whom I could become one. You wouldn't guess it to look at me but I'm a romantic. But it's getting rather late in the season for me. So, I'm inclined just to drift ... I don't have any problems getting through the night; it's the days that are so long and difficult now that spring is coming. Oh, spring is beautiful with the new buds on the trees and the bright sunshine, but it's such a melancholy season. It causes one to reflect ... Oh, but here I go, running off at the mouth again.

WEDNESDAY

Wednesday is named after Odin (Wotan) the chief of the Norse gods. Odin was in tough shape. He had an extremely difficult and painful education. He had one eye. He was anorexic and had a drinking problem. He had an eight-legged horse, a couple of wolves and two ravens, Thought and Memory, that flew all over the world but, presumably, returned to him on occasion.

The French word for Wednesday is *mercredi*, after the Roman god Mercury, a naked guy with wings on his heels, who went around delivering messages and flowers. He moved very quickly.

It is a windy, winter Wednesday as I write. Today is washday, there's a pot of beans boiling on the kitchen stove, steam condensing on the cold windowpanes. And today is the birthday of George Washington, the father of our country. "Wednesday's child is full of woe." So the nursery rhyme goes, but George Washington did all right, despite a couple of hard winters. Still, he was no barrel of laughs, either.

Wednesday is known as "hump day," halfway through the workweek, a hill from which you can view the road you are traveling, to where it vanishes in the haze at either horizon. On one side of the road trees in shadow, on the other trees in sun, and sometimes between the tall trunks, a glimpse of clear blue sky.

EXPANDING UNIVERSE

Not just the galaxies, everything is moving farther apart. That's why when I reached out for that glass it fell and shattered after a long, long fall to the floor. That is why I missed the first step going upstairs. And I so rarely see my friends anymore, seldom see them rise above the horizon: a distant glimmer in the darkening firmament. And you and I, are we moving apart as well? I smile and wink, wave to you there on the far side of the bed.

UP IN THE MORNING

"I don't belong here," I tell myself over and over. "I was never good at swimming and I have no sense of direction." Once again I'm lost and can't find the opening. I manage to breathe by sticking my nose into the little pockets of air just beneath the ice, gasping ...Then suddenly, by some miracle, over there, not fifty feet away, the light shining down from the other world. I haul my ass out onto the ice sheet. At last. I can warm my blubber in the sunshine, have a cup of coffee, some orange juice, maybe have one or two of those little almond cookies, read a bit of the newspaper, find out what's happening in New York and Los Angeles, perhaps even smoke a cigar before I'm noticed.

WRONG TURN

You missed your turn two miles back because you weren't paying attention: daydreaming. So now you have decided to turn here, on the wrong road, just because you are too lazy to turn around. You have decided to turn here just because of some vague notion. You have decided to turn here just because you aren't smart enough not to. You have decided to turn here ... just because. Listen, help is available. There are people who have experience with this kind of thing, people who have been through this. There are hotlines. There are brochures. There are programs, support groups. There is financial aid. Listen. The angels gather around you like gnats, strumming their guitars, singing songs of salvation, singing songs of freedom and diversity. But you aren't listening. Here you are on the genuine road less traveled. The road never snowplowed. Nothing to do but follow the ruts. Here the snow is too deep to turn around. You are going to have to follow this road to whatever nowhere it leads to.

Distance from the Sun

2004

SUITCASE

I keep my clothes in a suitcase at the foot of my bed. I haven't been anywhere and have no plans to go anywhere, but these days you never know, and besides it gives me a focus for my anxiety and for my occasional moments of unfounded excitement and anticipation. Every morning I take out clean socks and underwear, etc. and throw the dirty clothes back in the suitcase. Once a week or so I take the suitcase down to the washer and dryer in the basement and sit around naked waiting for my clean clothes. That's about it. The days pass quickly enough. Once in awhile I see old friends. "You look tired," they say or "Why the long face?" I reply, "Well, you know, it's stressful, living out of a suitcase."

North of the Cities

2007

LEGEND

As you grow older you begin to enter the world of myth, you become less a fact and more a legend. The word becomes flesh and then gradually becomes word once more. You exist mainly as the stories people tell about you, full of inconsistencies, inaccuracies and downright lies. Anything else, what's really happening, isn't very interesting. But then, the stories most people tell aren't that good either. You can see this. The lives of the people you know become harder and harder to believe.

WINTER DAY

It is one of those dark winter days with a heavy snow falling. I start to move a chair from its place in the corner and suddenly realize someone had been sitting there in the shadows all along. "Oh! I'm sorry!" "Oh, no problem," he says, as he jumps up. I try replacing the chair, but it's no use. He stands at the window, hands folded behind his back, watching the snow fall in the yard. "Would you like some tea?" "No, no, I'm fine." I feel as though I should know this person; that he is here out of some courtesy to me. "This snow is really coming down," he says. "Yes," I say. "I should be going before the roads get too bad." He stands at the window and does not move. "Yes," I say.

THE AFTERLIFE

Older people are exiting this life as if it were a movie ...
"I didn't get it," they are saying.

He says, "It didn't seem to have any plot."

"No," she says, "it seemed like things just kept coming at
me. Most of the time I was confused ... and there was way
too much sex and violence."

"Violence anyway," he says.

"It was not much for character development either; most
of the time people were either shouting or mumbling.
Then just when someone started to make sense and I got
interested, they died. Then a whole lot of new characters
came along and I couldn't tell who was who."

"The whole thing lacked subtlety."

"Some of the scenery was nice."

"Yes."

They walk on in silence for a while. It is a summer night
and they walk slowly, stopping now and then, as if they
had no particular place to go. They walk past a streetlamp
where some insects are hurling themselves at the light, and
then on down the block, fading into the darkness.

She says, "I was never happy with the way I looked."

"The lighting was bad and I was no good at dialogue,"
he says.

"I would have liked to have been a little taller," she says.

FIGURE STUDIES

What do you do when you want to write but can't think of a thing, not a word? I think composers have it better, they can at least play the scale if they can't think of a tune: do re mi fa ... A painter has all that color, and if you ran out of ideas, you could do yet another self-portrait, or get a model and do figure studies. Maybe that's what I need, a model, an attractive young woman. I'd say, "Lie down on that couch, my dear, open your dressing gown just a bit more. Like that, yes,"... and I would write in my notebook, "Your lips are like petals ... Your teeth are like the stars ..."

BIG BROWN PILLS

I believe in the big brown pills: they lower cholesterol and improve digestion. They help prevent cancer and build brain cells. Plus, they just make you feel better overall. I believe in coffee and beet greens and fish oil, of course, and red wine, in moderation, and cinnamon. Green tea is good and black tea and ginseng. I eat my broccoli. Nuts are very good, and dark chocolate—has to be dark, not milk chocolate. Tomatoes. But I think the big brown pills really help. I used to believe in the little yellow pills, but now I believe in the big brown pills. I believe that they are much more effective. I still take the little yellow ones, but I really believe in the big brown ones.

A NEW POEM

I am driving again, the back roads of northern Minnesota, on my way from A to B, through the spruce and tamarack. To amuse myself I compose a poem. It is the same poem I wrote yesterday, the same poem I wrote last week, the same poem I always write, but it helps to pass the time. It's September and everything has gone to seed, the maple leaves are beginning to turn and the warblers are on their way south. The tansy and goldenrod in the ditches are covered with dust. Already my hair has turned gray. The dark comes much earlier now. Soon winter will come. I sigh and wonder, where has the time gone?

LAW OF THE JUNGLE

We die of silliness, finally. Remember all those nights of wine, the heated discussion, the smoky room, the music? Those questions you pondered then have no relevance "Why do we live?" you asked. More to the point now is, "Where do I live?" First you forget to zip; then, as time goes by, you forget to unzip. There is a banana peel around every corner. Remember all those powerful, intense things you said back then, how the girls found you powerful and intense? You couldn't say those things with a straight face now, and anyway, those girls weren't really listening. The old lion, with patchy mane and sagging belly stands up to guard his territory. He gives a pathetic roar and the hyenas die laughing.

WHEN IT GETS COLD

When it gets cold around here we like to throw hot water into the air and watch it become instant ice mist that drifts away, never hitting the ground. Sometimes we drive nails with a frozen banana. Sometimes we just watch the numbers on the gas and the electric meters go spinning by. There's just no end to the fun.

But things get weird when it gets very cold. Things you never imagined come to life. There's an insect that appears, some kind of fly. Trees and houses make strange noises, and there are spooky, misty shapes moving around in the woods. Once when it was twenty-five below I found bare human footprints in snow that had fallen just a few hours before.

Everyone gets a little crazy when it's very cold for several weeks. Some people go in for compulsive house cleaning, others read, read everything: milk cartons, shipping labels ... We eat too much. We sleep a lot too. Once, during a cold spell, I slept for three days and when I woke I drank a gallon and a half of coffee.

AMBITION

One of the good things about getting older is that no one asks anymore "What are you going to be when you grow up?" Or later on, "What do you do?" Questions for which I never had a good answer. Nowadays everyone assumes I'm retired, and that I have no ambition whatsoever. It isn't true. It is true that it's too late for me to become an Olympic champion swimmer or a lumberjack, but my ambitions are on higher things. I want to be a cloud. I'm taking some classes and have a really good instructor. I don't want to be a threatening storm cloud, just one of those sunny summer clouds. Not that I won't have a dark side, of course. I'd like to be one of those big fat cumulus clouds that pass silently overhead on a beautiful day. A day so fine, in fact, that you might not even notice me, as I sailed over your town on my way somewhere else, but you'd feel good about it.

NONFICTION

I don't like it when someone else's fantasy world interferes with my own. That's why I don't read novels much anymore or watch television. I don't go for nonfiction either. Fiction and nonfiction aren't opposites. It isn't truth vs. lies. Nonfiction is simply not fiction—it's something else, I don't know what. Take the president, for example. From what I read in the newspapers, (which, as I am led to believe, are nonfiction) he can't be real. He has to be made up by some really bad writer. Unless I imagined all that stuff.

CLEAN UP

We invited some people over for drinks because they seemed nice and we thought it would be fun. They're about our age, a little younger maybe, and we have some things in common. They are coming this evening so now we have to clean the place up. What a drag. But we can't let them think that we are slobs, that we leave the morning oatmeal to dry hard in the pot, that the sink is full of yesterday's dirty dishes, that the kitchen table is piled high with books and magazines and coffee-stained papers, that the bed is unmade and the floor needs vacuuming. We can't let it appear that we are the kind of people who forget to change the car oil or mow the goddamn lawn; that we have completely lost our grip. We want them to know that we have not succumbed, that we can maintain order in the midst of all this chaos.

A PLACE OF YOUR OWN

It is so good to have a place of your own, a comfortable bed, a place where in the evening you can hide away from all the defeat of the day, a place where you know where things are, or at least you know in which pile a particular item might be found. But suppose one day the place gets ransacked while you are away. Maybe you're lucky, maybe it was only the three bears, but the place is a mess, your neat stack of L.L. Bean catalogs strewn all over. They've eaten everything; even that jar of pickled Brussels spouts way at the back of the fridge. Even after you get it all cleaned up it's not the same as it was. "You have to move on," a friend of mine says, "at our age we can just close the door and go away, take a trip to China or Hot Springs. Just think of it as practice for not being here at all."

EVOLUTION

I think it's okay not to like the idea of evolution. I can understand how one would not like to think of oneself as distantly related to a lemur, since most of us are none too fond of some of our more immediate relatives. But it seems to me that evolution is the least of our worries. For years I have accepted things as they are, or seem to be, without thinking much about them. Not now. Now, I have come to realize that I don't approve of gale-force winds or high water, or volcanoes or earthquakes. The idea of tectonic plates doesn't appeal to me. The idea that we are dependent on gravity to keep us on the ground makes me queasy—the idea that there is no up or down and we are merely sticking out from the planet. I don't at all like the idea of flight, except for birds. I don't even enjoy riding in automobiles. I believe, even though I do not practice it, that we should walk everywhere we go. But then there's the problem of standing, balance and all that. I'm not so sure that just two legs is a good idea.

WHERE WE LIVE

It's easy to get lost in the woods around here, to wander around in circles, not 50 feet away from the path and never see it. Beneath the canopy of trees not even your GPS will work. It leads to a lot of uncertainty. So if you come to visit I can't be very specific with my directions. I can only give you probabilities. We leave a lot of notes around as indicators: "Dentist Thur. 9:30," "Eggs," "Pick up Mom." It doesn't always work. "Honey, what's this blank Post-It note stuck to the bathroom mirror all about?" "Oh, nothing," she says.

PARSIMONIOUS

What a luxury, what a gift to have had a life, more or less my own, to wander, la-de-da, beneath the quaking aspen with leaves like $100 gold pieces and the blue, blue sky. And what shall I do with such riches? Give them away. Give them parsimoniously to family and friends, to those I love and those who love me, and give them in great abundance to strangers: thieves, con artists, drunks, politicians; wastrels like myself.

SPIDER

An entrepreneurial spider has built her web between the bars of the railing at the scenic overlook in order to catch small insects blown in on the lake wind. If you can stick around she'll tell you all about the difficulties of owning a small business.

STARFISH

It seems like starfish don't do anything, but actually they move along at a rate of about 60 feet per hour. A starfish will eat anything that moves slower than it does, which excludes a great number of dishes from its diet. A starfish is all arms and appetite; it has no brain, yet in spite of this, time-lapse photography has shown that the starfish maintains an active social life. So in these regards the starfish is like many of the people you know.

EARL

In Sitka, because they are fond of them, people have named the sea lions. Every sea lion is named Earl because they are killed one after another by the orca, the killer whale; sea lion bodies tossed left and right into the air. "At least he didn't get Earl," someone says. And sure enough, after a time, that same friendly, bewhiskered face bobs to the surface. It's Earl again. Well, how else are you to live except by denial, by some palatable fiction, some little song to sing while the inevitable, the black and white blindsiding fact, comes hurtling toward you out of the deep?

SEAGULLS

There were no seagulls in the harbor, none at the marina. I saw none in the air. There were no seagulls at Canal Park, or McDonald's, or at Russ Kendall's smokehouse, or at the Kmart parking lot, or any of their favorite hangouts. It's winter and snow is falling, but I don't believe seagulls fly south. I've often seen them standing around on the ice all day, as if they were waiting for a big bus to come and take them to a casino. Where are all the seagulls? This is not a question I ever thought I'd ask myself. You get used to someone being around and if they go away you miss them. That's how life is. But seagulls are primarily a nuisance, and if you can't count on that, what can you count on?

LARGE DOG

A dog would be the thing, she thought, now that she lived alone, a big dog that looked rather scary and barked, a watchdog, but one that was actually gentle, a companion, a big, lovable fur ball. She adopted a dog from the pound, Walter, who was part German shepherd and part golden retriever. She got all his shots and had him neutered. She got a retractable leash for walks, morning and evening, after work. Walk time. Walter is happy, sniffing and pulling this way and that. She calls and pulls back. She has a big dog on a leash but she is going where he wants to go.

HORSE

It was probably a collection of human vices that led to the domestication of the horse: *envy* (I wish I could run that fast), *laziness* (if I rode on the back of the horse it would be much easier than walking), *greed* (just think how many rabbits I could kill), *vanity* (just think how good I'd look, all in black, on the back of that great white stallion). It took a brave soul to be the first one to ride a horse. He or she, no doubt, approached the horse slowly, whispering, "Nice horsey, here is a carrot for you. I'm going climb very gently and carefully onto your back and if you throw me off I'm going to hit you over your big stupid head with this big oak board." Having been a passenger on a horse once or twice, I understand the rush to invent the automobile. Nowadays the horse is ridden mostly for pleasure, if you can call it that. Personally, I prefer to watch horses: powerful bays and sorrels, pintos and roans running, muscles rippling, running across the plains, over the hills and far away.

BOWERBIRD

The satin bowerbird builds his bower carefully, a construction of twigs and grass, and carefully decorates it with display items, blue feathers, blue bottle caps, blue bits of paper and potsherds. His feathers are blue and he likes blue, and more to the point, the female bowerbird likes blue. During the mating season the bower is constantly rearranged and rebuilt. The bower isn't a nest, it's an elaborate construction designed to lure female bowerbirds. So it's like theoretical physics or poetry, hard work and essentially useless, except for the sex. And in most cases the female bowerbird doesn't even take a second look at what she considers to be a second-rate bower. She has an eye. She knows immediately a bower worthy of her close inspection. The bower builder is preening and doing his little song and dance. "You wouldn't believe how far I had to fly with that bottle cap in my beak." She likes the look of this bower, likes the way those twigs are arranged, just so. Likes the little touches of red plastic, here and there among the blue things. Yes, this is a bird that can build a better bower, should she ever need one. So perhaps she'll just step inside.

BAT

There's a bat circling in the early dark, between the pine tree, the spruce and the maple. He seems happy enough gobbling up perhaps hundreds of mosquitoes on each turn around. But maybe it's Dracula. You have to think about that. Maybe Dracula doesn't transform himself into bat; instead maybe the bat becomes Dracula. He has to go home soon, put on his little suit and tie and wander around the empty castle muttering to himself in a strange accent. And later, of course, there will be guests for dinner.

SQUIRREL

The squirrel makes a split-second decision and acts on it immediately—headlong across the street as fast as he can go. Sure, it's fraught with danger, sure there's a car coming, sure it's reckless and totally unnecessary, but the squirrel is committed. He will stay the course.

FISH/FISHERMAN

The fish are either off or on. Day after day there are no fish, only wind and waves, and seagulls waiting patiently. Then the fish are on. They come from nowhere, suddenly alive and turning and flashing in unison, uncles, cousins, daughters. All fish are one fish but their combined intelligence cannot outwit a gill net. Then the fish are off and lie in the bottom of the boat with x's for eyes.

After I've cleaned the fish and sold most of the day's catch, I bring a few home for supper. I always put one fish out on the stump beside the shed. In the morning the fish is gone. I don't know what takes it, if it's a weasel or a raccoon or a bear or a crow. I don't watch, or try to track whatever it is. I put the fish out in the evening, and in the morning it's gone.

ART

I decided that it would be nice to be someone else for a change. I call myself Art. Being someone else is kind of like having a guest, so my job is to make Art feel welcome and happy. What would Art like? Art would like coffee, I think, so off I go. When I meet someone I say "How do you do? Name's Art." If I meet someone I know already they say, "Your name is Lou, not Art, you have always been Lou." "Oh, all right then, call me Lou." (Art is a very easy-going guy.) I just don't see why people have to be so inflexible, so unequivocal, so ... definite. Meanwhile, I have learned that Art likes baseball, so I've got a ticket to this afternoon's Twins game.

CHAMELEON

I used to have a girlfriend named Jane Kieffer, from San Diego. She was beautiful and she was a chameleon. She could appear to be a small and waif-like blond or a tall redhead, to suit her whim, or mine. She would change her style, her look, her demeanor, almost instantly it seemed. She could be sophisticated or earthy, depending on my momentary needs, and the surroundings. She was fantastic, great at parties and when we were alone. She always knew just the right moves. The trouble was I didn't know what I wanted. It seemed, as a couple, we lacked any focus, any stability. She began to anticipate my moods and change in advance. It drove me crazy. "Who are you, why are you like this?" I asked. She said she was born in the sea and that she had no soul. "What about me?" "You have none either," she said. I was often angry and she would cry, or worse, sit impassively and say nothing, blending into the background. One day I pulled on my pants and said, "That's it. I'm leaving." I never saw her again—or else we got married and raised a family. I'm not sure.

DON'T GET AROUND MUCH ANYMORE

"Barbara, it is so good to see you! How are you getting along since your divorce?" "Why, Ellen, my divorce was twenty years ago! I'm fine."

"No! Twenty years, it can't have been that long?"

"Yes."

"How are your children?"

"They're both doing well, Jeff lives in Seattle and works for Microsoft. He and his wife have two boys, Evan and Lyle. Lyle is still in high school and Evan is in his second year at MIT studying engineering. Mara lives in Chicago and works for an ad agency. She's doing well, she and her partner are remodeling an old farmhouse near Oshkosh, so she's very busy, all that driving back and forth."

"And how about yourself, Barbara?"

"Oh, I'm very busy as well, work at the church, I work with the AAUW and I still play golf when I can."

"That's so good Barb! I think it's important to stay involved after a divorce. It's been so good to see you and remember, Barb, these things just take time."

MARRIAGE

He said "People say marriage is like a three-legged race, but in our case she and I are tied together facing in the opposite directions on the stairs—she heading toward the main floor with the carpets and the furniture and such, and me heading to the basement with the furnace and the laundry tubs. It's okay, we get along, going nowhere, but it's damned difficult for the children or anyone else to get by us, whichever way they are headed."

THE COMMON COLD

It was something you said, no doubt, while half asleep. Some meaningless rant that took on a life of its own. That someone breathed in, misunderstood, and breathed out. That mutated like all gossip, that went away and was gone for years, prodigal son working at the pizza parlor, accumulating a list of grudges, never getting the respect he thought was his due, and every day planning his return.

THE RAVEN

"I'm really a princess," the raven said from its perch on a pine branch. "Really?" I said, acting as though I was not all surprised to be conversing with a raven.

"My evil stepmother put a curse on me. A spell that can only be broken by a prince. I can see from here that you are no prince. Do you happen to be a wizard?"

"No, I'm sorry."

"I just thought, since you have this little shack in the woods, you might be a wizard. I had a wizard once, not a very good wizard I'm afraid. He was the one who told me that I'd need a prince, a prince who loved me and would perform all kinds of difficult and time-consuming tasks. These tasks involved giants, gloomy forests, castles, high mountains, that sort of thing. I must have gone through half-a-dozen princes and none of them were up to it. Most of them turned out to be toads. They all married commoners and live really dull-normal lives now. Then one day I found my man. He was handsome, he was crazy about me, and he would do anything for me, slay dragons, sail the widest seas ... But when he had finished all the tasks ... nothing. Nothing changed! I was still a raven. There were accusations, recriminations. The prince said I'd tricked him, that I wasn't really a princess. I said he'd never even seen a dragon let alone slain one. We had a bitter parting. I flew back to find the wizard but he'd gone out of business. Moved. No forwarding address. I searched for a year, even hired a private investigator, but never found him. I don't suppose he could have helped me anyway. He was a lousy wizard. I've been a raven so long now that I've almost gotten used to it ... Are you sure you aren't a wizard?"

"I'm sure. Just a guy who has a shack in the woods."
"You don't have a cloak that makes you invisible?"
"No."
"No seven league boots?"
"No."
"How about a dead rabbit then?"

IF IT WAS A SNAKE

You've lost something, your car keys, or your watch and you have searched for what seems like hours. But then suddenly it appears, right there on the table, not two feet away. "If it was a snake it would have bit you," Mother said. That's what you remember, a phrase, an old saying. My sister said, "Grandma told me, 'Never wear horizontal stripes, they make you look fat.' That's one of the few things I remember about Grandma." Or the words disappear and an image remains. I was getting a lecture from my parents about riding my tricycle all the way downtown. I don't remember anything they said. I remember looking out the window, it was just dark, and a block away a man wearing a white shirt and a tie passed under the streetlight and vanished into the night. That's all. Out of a lifetime, a few words, a few pictures, and everything you have lost is lurking there in the dark, poised to strike.

UNCLE AXEL

In the box of old photos there's one of a young man with a moustache wearing a long coat, circa 1890. The photo is labeled "Uncle Karl" on the back. That would be your mother's granduncle, who came from Sweden, a missionary, and was killed by Indians in North Dakota, your great-granduncle. The young man in the photo is looking away from the camera, slightly to the left. He has a look of determination, a man of destiny, preparing to bring the faith to the heathen Sioux. But it isn't Karl. The photo was mislabeled, fifty years ago. It's actually a photo of Uncle Axel, from Norway, your father's uncle, who was a farmer. No one knows that now. No one remembers Axel, or Karl. If you look closely at the photo it almost appears that the young man is speaking, perhaps muttering "I'm Axel damn it. Quit calling me Karl!"

GREAT GRAY OWL

In fact, he does not care who you are. He does know that you are not to be trusted. He fixes you with his yellow-eyed stare, unapologetic, unafraid. This is the extent of the wisdom he has to offer. Any questions you may have you will have to answer for yourself.

III.

BALONEY

There's a young couple in the parking lot, kissing. Not just kissing, they look as though they might eat each other up, kissing, nibbling, biting, mouths wide open, play fighting like young dogs, wrapped around each other like snakes. I remember that, sort of, that hunger, that passionate intensity. And I get a kind of nostalgic craving for it, in the way that I get a craving, occasionally, for the food of my childhood. Baloney on white bread, for instance: one slice of white bread with mustard or Miracle Whip or ketchup—not ketchup, one has to draw the line somewhere—and one slice of baloney. It had a nice symmetry to it, the circle of baloney on the rectangle of bread. Then you folded the bread and baloney in the middle and took a bite out of the very center of the folded side. When you unfolded the sandwich you had a hole, a circle in the center of the bread and baloney frame, a window, a porthole from which you could get a new view of the world.

THE BIG BANG

When the morning comes that you don't wake up, what remains of your life goes on as some kind of electromagnetic energy. There's a slight chance you might appear on someone's screen as a dot. Face it. You are a blip or a ping, part of the background noise, the residue of the Big Bang. You remember the Big Bang, don't you? You were about 26 years old, driving a brand new red and white Chevy convertible, with that beautiful blond girl at your side, Charlene, was her name. You had a case of beer on ice in the back, cruising down Highway number 7 on a summer afternoon and then you parked near Loon Lake just as the moon began to rise. Way back then you said to yourself, "Boy, it doesn't get any better than this," and you were right.

PLANTING

I am not planting an acorn from which a mighty and symbolic oak will grow. There is no time for that now. I'll just plant a few seeds, a row of nasturtiums perhaps. I'm not looking for a career. I missed that. I just want a part-time job, nothing too strenuous. Because this isn't about growth or beauty or meaning, it's about the question of whether, at my age, having gotten down in the literal and metaphorical dirt, I can get up again.

FREEZE

Everything in the garden is dead, killed by a sudden hard freeze, the beans, the tomatoes, fruit still clinging to the branches. It's all heaped up ready to go to the compost pile: rhubarb leaves, nasturtiums, pea vines, even the geraniums. It's too bad. The garden was so beautiful, green and fresh, but then we were all beautiful once. Everything dies, we understand. But the mind of the observer, which cannot imagine not imagining, goes on. The dynasties are cut down like the generations of grass, the bodies blacken and turn into coal. The waters rise and cover the earth and the mind broods on the face of the deep, and learns nothing.

MUSHROOM HUNTING

Here I am, as usual, wandering vaguely through a dark wood. Just when I think I know something, when I think I have discerned some pattern, a certain strategy—ah, they grow on the north edge of the low mossy spots—I find one on top of a rise and it shoots my theory all to hell. Every time I find one it's a surprise. The truth is there is no thought that goes into this. These things just pop up. And all this thinking, this human consciousness, isn't what it's cracked up to be. Some inert matter somehow gets itself together, pokes itself up from the ground, gets some ideas and goes walking around, wanting and worrying, gets angry, takes a kick at the dog and falls apart.

THE GREAT PLAINS

I was born around here. It's difficult to pinpoint the exact location because it's all the same, the big empty middle of the country. Over here it's flat as a tabletop, and here it's more rolling. Here's corn, and over there wheat, but don't bother with nuances, really it's all the same. It's cattle and oil. It's "Howdy Jesus! Gimme a Coors." It's wind and dust and tumbleweeds. It's 500 miles before the sun goes down: one little town after another. "How far is it from Cargill to Monsanto Falls?" What do people do here? They live here, same as people live anywhere. They die here too.

Once some friends and I organized a poetry reading tour of regional cemeteries, funded by a grant from the State Arts Board, to pay for the gasoline and the booze. It was an effort to bring some culture to the area. The audiences were not the most responsive. However, I took the fact that there was no coughing or shuffling during my readings as a sign of interest and attentiveness.

THINGS DON'T GO

Things don't go the way you want them to go. If you think the handle turns to the right, it turns to the left. Whichever way you think it turns; it turns the other way. It is no use trying to anticipate this; in every case it goes the other way. There's no use looking for your hat, it's on your head, where you will never see it. Whatever comes to you comes as a gift without your name on it. The moon wanders around the night sky, the sun rises, and a flock of birds lands briefly in the unmown grass.

CROSSROAD BLUES

As these things go, there are no other cars on the road for miles and we arrive simultaneously at the four-way stop at the junction of the Munger-Shaw Road and Yggdrasill Road, he in his big four-by-four Ford pickup and me in my beat-up old Chrysler. Because I'm feeling magnanimous and he's on my right, I motion to him to go ahead. Then he waves me to go first. Then we both start and both come to a sudden halt. I motion again for him to go. Then the son-of-a-bitch flips me the bird. Well, screw you mister, and I flip him the bird right back. Neither of us moves. One of us has to go first but I'll be damned if it's going to be me.

ILLUSION

Is it true that this world, this life, is an illusion, all smoke and mirrors? It must be, because according to a recent poll, seventy percent of the American public believes that Ronald Reagan did a good job as president. And yet if life is only a figment, a feint, a construction of breath and vapor, then why is it a rock falls and smashes your toe and you go hopping around on one foot, mad with pain? Why, if you happen to look at a woman on the sidewalk and your car plows into the truck in front of you, are you dead and no longer allowed to play the game? It's an illusion, but it's a damn good one.

SPIRIT WIND

Car headlights come rushing up from behind, someone doing 80 on this lonely back road then, just as they get within a hundred yards of the car, the headlights vanish. He couldn't have turned ... And there was the time when something—there was no wind, no one inside the house— slammed the door just as you were about to enter. There is something out there, no doubt, something that defies explanation and that does not necessarily wish you well. But it's best not to go giving it dumb names like "Spirit Wind." Best not say anything about it at all; just keep your big mouth shut. Like that little yellow bird, for instance. I've seen it, tiny yellow bird that flies in and out of your ear. Perhaps it nests there in the top of a tiny banana tree. And when your new lover leans forward for the first time to kiss your delicate shell-like ear, he says, "You've got a banana tree in your ear!" "What?" you say, "I can't hear you ..."

MY POEM

I am so pleased that you brought this in. What you have is a masterpiece of its kind: genuine, handcrafted, poetry—I'd say late twentieth century, truly a remarkable work. We here agree that its value, conservatively, is from ten to twelve thousand dollars. But, on a good day with the right buyer it could fetch upwards of fifteen thousand, although the market for this kind of thing is a bit soft right now. Now, you have told me that you will never sell this piece and I think that that is a good idea. However, if I were in the insurance business, I would advise you to insure this fine work for at least thirty thousand dollars. And remember to keep it out of direct sunlight.

COLORS

She said, "I see people as colors. My friend Jenny is yellow or gold." "Because she is blond?" "No it's not that. I think of James, for instance, as black, like a pirate flag, but his hair is quite blond." James was my rival, two years older and in college. "What color are you?" "Oh, I'm spring colors; maybe that bright green that you see when the leaves are still small. Kind of young and dumb." She laughed. She was so beautiful, her hair a wonderful red-gold and her eyes, I thought, green as the spring leaves. I knew I was getting nowhere. "What about me?" I asked. "What color am I?" "Oh, I see you as brown," she said, "shades of brown."

A DISAPPOINTMENT

The best anyone can say about you is that you are a disappointment. We had higher expectations of you. We had hoped that you would finish your schooling. We had hoped that you would have kept your job at the plant. We had hoped that you would have been a better son and a better father. We hoped, and fully expected, that you would finish reading *Moby Dick*. I wish that, when I am talking to you, you would at least raise your head off your desk and look at me. There are people who, without your gifts, have accomplished so much in this life. I am truly disappointed. Your parents, your wife and children, your entire family, in fact, everyone you know is disappointed, deeply disappointed.

A VISIT TO JUNEAU

Juneau is a noisy place in summer, cruise boats arriving and departing, airplanes landing and taking off, seaplanes coming and going, helicopters all in a row—off to look at the glacier. There are fishing boats bringing in their catch, chum salmon doing belly flops in the harbor, automobiles racing around—even though there is really no place you can get to by car. There are people selling jewelry and furs and popcorn and there are tourists everywhere. For a long time this whole area was covered in ice and it was quiet and the big mountains looked silently down on the sea. None of this activity makes any sense, but this is what we do. Apparently, this is our job. So when some guy calls me and wants me to move his refrigerator and paint the floor underneath, it's okay with me.

WISHES

Wishes, if they come true, always have a way of turning out badly. The fisherman's wife got wealth and power but wound up with nothing. Tithonus was given eternal life by Zeus but not eternal youth so the gift had unpleasant consequences. King Midas did not do well with his wish either. Solomon wished for wisdom, got wealth and power besides and still was not a happy man. Suppose you wished to be far away from the stupid, repressive town you grew up in and suddenly you were whirled away in a cloud of dust. Before long some well-intentioned fool would miss you and wish you home again. If you wished for a beautiful woman or rich and handsome husband you know what would happen. What is there to wish for finally? A blindfold and a last cigarette? No, we all know how bad smoking is for your health. When the genie comes out of the bottle or the man comes to your door with a check the size of a billboard you should say "No." "No thank you." Say, "I don't want any." Say, "I wish you would go away." But you aren't going to, are you?

WORRY BEADS

for Dennis Matson

The hand is held outward, away from the body in the gesture of one about to shake the hand of another. The string of the worry beads is held between the first and second fingers, at approximately the middle joint of the fingers. The string is attached to a loop of metal beads, which hangs down on the outside of the hand. The loop is flipped up and over the hand with a quick outward motion of the little finger and without turning the wrist. The beads now hang on the inside of the hand. They are now flipped back to their original position with the thumb. Thus to (theoretically) relieve tension and anxiety this action is repeated rapidly many times. After repeated attempts I find I am unable to do this and it worries me.

EUROPEAN SHOES

2008

Preface

This book is loosely based on my European travels in late summer and fall of 2007, along with a few prose poems. It is useless as a travel guide and offers no insight whatsoever into European art, culture, politics or daily life.

Louis Jenkins

Prose Poems

NEW SHOES

Because I'm in Europe, I've been thinking of buying some European shoes. European shoes do not look quite like American shoes. You look at someone's shoes and say to yourself, "those are European shoes. They are made of leather, the toes are more pointy, or more square, or ... something ... they are just different." In America we mostly wear tennis shoes. We have casual tennis shoes, formal tennis shoes, even tennis shoes for tennis. Over here it is different, but my eye is not practiced enough to determine if the shoes vary from country to country. If that is the case, and since all shoes are made in China, think how confusing it must be for the Chinese worker packaging up the shoes for shipment, looking at a pair of loafers, scratching his or her head and wondering "Do these shoes go to Luxembourg or Hungary?" In China, as we all know, everyone wears silk bedroom slippers.

HANS BRINKER

We are sitting at an outdoor café, drinking and watching the bicycles pass silently by on the other side of the canal. It is dusk and a young guy pedals by with his girl riding sidesaddle on the back. There are bicycles everywhere, bicycles being ridden and bicycles parked in bicycle parking lots, hundreds and hundreds. Some look as though they have been parked for twenty or thirty, maybe fifty years. We are sitting with friends discussing Hans Brinker; "Was he the boy who put his finger in the dike?" "No, no— silver skates." "Didn't he get silver skates for putting his finger in the dike?" No one knows.

Sometime after the Second World War, in the early 1950's, Hans Brinker rode his silver bicycle home from his job at the tulip farm smoking a doobie, parked in a nearby bicycle lot and went into Windmill Tavern for some fresh herring and a few beers. During a brawl that began as an argument over the proper construction of dikes, Hans got hit over the head with a wooden shoe and died. Because Hans was a bachelor and had no living relatives the bicycle was forgotten. Today it is still there, somewhere amongst a thousand other bicycles, slowly rusting away.

FREYA GOES SHOPPING

Nobody thinks about how difficult it is to embody all beauty, sexual desire, hope, love, domestic bliss and wild runaway passion; in short to represent some wide-ranging, out of control, hormonal brush fire. Everyone thinks *what a great job*. But no one understands what it means to be a symbol, a deity. It's way worse than being merely a queen, or a movie star, I can tell you. My own feelings are never considered. I have no private life. I'm too busy being some kind of universal principle. No one wonders if this is what I really want, if this is right for me. Well, come Friday I'm taking off. I'm going to have some quality time: my time, my place, my self. I may do some shopping at *The Dwarves*. They have some beautiful things. They have a necklace down there made of rubies and amber that is to die for. And it would go so nicely with that earth-red shawl I have. They have an outrageous price on that necklace but I know those guys, and I know what they want.

IN OSLO

All she has to do is look at you, that's all, and you fall hopelessly in love. If she should touch your hand you would turn to jello, you would begin to speak in tongues. Whatever you were doing, wherever you were going, that's all over now. She is the only star on your horizon, the sole bright light in the perfect blue evening sky.

But she doesn't look at you. She strides down Karl Johan's Gate with her tall boots and her flowing blond hair, talking on her mobile and she does not see you. You may as well be a kiosk with all your silly love poems flapping in the breeze, just another object to be maneuvered around. And it's a good thing too, if she looked straight at you, you would probably drop dead right here in the street.

MY ANCESTRAL HOME

We came to a beautiful little farm. From photos I'd seen I knew this was the place. The house and barn were painted in the traditional Falu red, trimmed with white. It was nearly midsummer, the trees and grass, lush green. When we arrived the family was gathered at a table on the lawn for coffee and fresh strawberries. Introductions were made all around, Grandpa Sven, Lars-Olaf and Marie, Eric and Gudren, Cousin Inge and her two children ... It made me think of a Carl Larsson painting. But, of course, it was all modern, the Swedes are very up-to-date, Lars-Olaf was an engineer for Volvo, and they all spoke perfect English, except for Grandpa, and there was a great deal of laughter over my attempts at Swedish. We stayed for a long time laughing and talking, it was late in the day but the sun was still high. I felt a wonderful kinship. It seemed to me that I had known these people all my life, they even looked like family back in the States. But as it turned out we had come to the wrong farm. Lars-Olaf said, "I think I know your people, they live about three miles from here. If you like I could give them a call." I said that no, that it wasn't necessary, this was close enough.

FROM THE TRAIN

It was the backyard of some little house in a poor neighborhood at the edge of the city. The lawn was green and seemed well cared for, even though the yard was right next to the main track. Then I noticed two people in the yard, a man and a woman (of course) and they seemed at first to be wrestling, crouched facing each other and their hands gripping either each other's or some object. Or was it a child? Were they angry or was this just a playful moment? Were they struggling with some home-improvement project, trying to move a recalcitrant cement birdbath? I couldn't really see and we passed so quickly. In only moments we were passing some small factories and sidetracks where there were what seemed like acres of rusting railway car wheels.

EMPLOYMENT OPPORTUNITIES AT NORWICH CATHEDRAL 1408

Son, it's about time you followed me down to work at the church. You're a good strong lad and I've taught you well and we can use another hand working on the transept. "Father, I have spoken with Wat le Glaysner and he is willing to take me as an apprentice. Father, I want to go into stained glass." Stained glass?! Oh well, aren't we something? Stained glass is it? My, my ... Well let me tell you boy, we Greebes have always been stone masons, your grandfather was a stone mason working at the church and his father and his father's father, all working at the church, 300 years or more and it's not done yet. So don't you go talking to me about stained glass. You take up your hammer and chisel and get to work.

FULL ENGLISH BREAKFAST

One fried egg.

One English-style sausage (terrible, full of some bread-like substance. Also called a banger because of their tendency to explode during cooking).

Two rashers of crispy fried bacon (good).

A portion of fried mushrooms.

One slice of fried black pudding (a type of sausage made with pig's blood).

One slice of fried white pudding (same as above, I think, except without the blood. Both of these are better than you might imagine).

Half a tomato, fried until brown (this is OK if it's a fresh tomato and not a canned one, as it sometimes is).

One slice of fried bread (a slice of white bread fried in oil, preferably bacon fat)

Possible options:

Hash browns

Bubble and squeak (chief ingredients are potato and cabbage, but carrots, peas, Brussels sprouts, other left-over vegetables can be added. The cold chopped vegetables are fried in a pan together with mashed potato until the mixture is well cooked and brown on the sides).

Beans (often canned pork n' beans).

Marmite (stuff to spread on your fried bread. The British version of the product is a sticky, dark brown paste with a distinctive, powerful flavor, which is extremely salty and somewhat like soy sauce. This distinctive taste is reflected in the British company's marketing slogan: "Love it or hate it.").

Marmalade (also for your bread, also an acquired taste in
   my opinion but I tasted some that was homemade
   by a friend that was excellent)
Tea.

OUT OF IT

I'm out of it these days. I guess I have less interest in
keeping up to date on what's happening. I don't know
the names of most of the current movie stars and have not
seen their movies. Same for the music scene. I have not
read what everyone is reading. I don't know what's on
TV. I'm out of it, but not too far out. I figure somewhere
between 12 and 18 inches. I've noticed that when someone
speaks to me he or she seems to be addressing a space
just a little to my right or left. When it first happened I
thought my acquaintance was speaking to someone else. I
looked around but there was no one else there. I've tried
moving to adjust the conversational direction but the
speaker only readjusts. I realized that if I kept moving our
conversation would be going in concentric circles. So now
I just stand still and let the talk continue at cross-purposes.
It is getting worse. Sometimes I can't make any sense at all
of what someone is saying, as if he were speaking Welsh.
Then I remember that I am in Wales and he is speaking
Welsh.

A CLASSIC TALE

I fell deeply in love with the frail girl. Something about her, her courage, her strength in adversity, aroused in me a deep tenderness I had not known before. I would put my arms around her and ask, "Are you warm enough?" How wonderful it was to hear her laugh when I made jokes. She loved me, as well, despite the difference in our ages, or in some ways because of it. Perhaps it was because of a certain perverseness in her nature. She knew that, due to my age and background, I was the one person to whom her parents would most object. Perhaps that and the little stir we caused wherever we went, the things whispered about us, combined with her illness drove her to love me with a feverish passion. The reasons did not matter to me. Her mother hated me with equal passion. She was jealous, certainly, of me and of the lavish attention I received from her daughter but, I think, jealous of her daughter as well, jealous of her happiness. When finally the guise of politeness was dropped her mother said, "Can't you see this is all wrong? Leave her alone, she's young, she deserves a life, a man of her own age." I said "Madam, your daughter has honored me with her love and I will not betray that honor. No one has your daughter's welfare more in mind and no one loves her more than I." "You? You vain, arrogant old fool! Don't you realize you have been dead for fifty years?"

WAKING AT NIGHT

One of those angels of death appears, the kind that are common as telemarketers, or Jehovah's Witnesses, and for some reason this one speaks with a German accent: "Morgen."

"No, Jenkins"

"Louise?" He's reading from a card.

"No, Louise is a female name, I'm male."

"We are blind to gender, race, color, nationality, religion or sexual orientation."

"Nevertheless, you came for a specific person and it isn't me, so goodbye ... and don't let the door hit you in the ass on the way out. (I said this last part under my breath.)

If you wake in the night you'll be able to get back to sleep if you can make it to the bathroom and back to bed without thinking of anything. I have no problem with this, and I bet you won't either.

AMERICAN ABROAD

I'm the guy they call when no one else knows what to do. To be more specific I'm the guy they call when no one else realizes that anything needs to be done. I specialize in potential problem identification, part of a program we have called Problem Investigation: Suggestions and Solutions. It's a growing field. My clients range from big, high-tech companies right down to local arts organizations. I love my job. I graduated from college ten years ago with a degree in Business Education. I worked at Burger King for a year, then I ran a tanning salon for a couple years. I got my certificate from the Human Discovery Institute five years ago and worked for them for a while before I went free-lance. The business has really taken off since. I'm on the road most of the year. I feel like I should spend more time at home since my kids are still young and my wife would like more help. But I can't really afford to take time off. It's a dilemma. Right now, for instance, I'm advising certain high-level political figures, very important stuff that I'm not at liberty to talk about, and that really keeps me busy.

PORTRAIT OF A LADY

I know her, and really, she doesn't look that good. Her nose is bigger than that. It's a good thing she wasn't painted in profile. I knew her before she was a Lady, but I won't go into that. She married well, minor nobility, Viscount Somethingorother. I know the painter as well, Carlos Whathisname—Spanish guy, a real party animal, used to hang out with Watteau and that bohemian crowd. This was a good gig for him, the portrait. Because the viscount was absolutely gaga about his wife and money was no problem for him. I must say Carlos did a good job, the highlights on the dress and all. I think originally he had the estate in the background but changed the painting to focus on his subject, and he got it; that way she has of seeming to be looking right at you—but she isn't really.

COTE D'AZUR

I am living in a small rented room on the Rue Merde du Chien. I am at work on my book of poems, which I will dedicate to you. I have had to pawn my iPhone in order to buy bread. But it is of no importance since you no longer call or even text.

Every morning I walk down to the sea, and in the evening I walk back to my room with my baguette where I am greeted by the concierge, who regards me with suspicion. Even after all these months my French is not good. "Bonsoir madam" "Bonsoir monsieur." So why do I stay, you ask? Perhaps it is because I have no place to go, or because I have so little money and so little ambition... But I believe it is because of the sea, the sea holds me here, the sea so blue, the Cote d'Azur. Everyday I write in my notebook. "Today the sea is so blue, as blue as your eyes." Or "The sea is blue today but not as blue as your eyes." Or "The sea is more blue than your eyes." It does not go well. Yesterday I wrote, "The sea is dark and troubled today." But it is not true ... it is just the sea.

THE SILK ROAD

We wouldn't have to go home. We could go on from here to Istanbul, then to Ankara and Tabriz, over the Silk Road. It will probably take months, years maybe, on foot or camelback to reach Xian. We'd go through Theran, Asgabat, Bukhara, Samarkand, Tashkent, Kashgar, Turphan, Hami, Anxi, Lanzhou. Across deserts, rivers and mountains. We'd see the Great Wall, Maiji Mountain, Jiayuguan Pass, Wuwei Confucius Temple. It worries me a bit that we have nothing to trade. The Chinese have silk, gunpowder ...They like horses I guess ... Maybe we could pick up some frankincense and myrrh along the way but I'm not exactly sure where you get that stuff or if I'd know it when I saw it. I don't see this as a big problem though, we'll just go along and things will occur as they occur. Tonight ... perhaps Venice or Trieste.

Prose

A Travel Journal

2007. August 15. At 2:00 PM we attempt to catch a taxi from the Brooklyn Museum of Art to the Brooklyn Cruise Terminal where we will board the Queen Mary 2. Brooklyn is not full of taxis like Manhattan. You have to call a car service. With the help of a kindly museum guard we finally get a car (black, not yellow) and in ten minutes we are at the terminal. Then it's standing in line, x-ray luggage inspection, etc. "Have you been sick—vomiting, diarrhea?" No. More waiting, paperwork ... then finally we are aboard, in our "stateroom" which is perfectly nice, with a balcony, only we have a view of a lifeboat. Ours is an "obstructed view," which saves us a lot of money, and besides, I figure my view is usually obstructed. We will have plenty of ocean viewing. Next is lifeboat drill— assemble on deck 8, lifejacket instruction. At five o'clock we are underway. No cheering crowds, no crepe paper streamers, but we do have a police boat and helicopter escort, past Ellis Island, past the Statue of Liberty out into the Atlantic, on and on, into the dark.

August 18. 11:09 AM (7:09 AM Duluth time) We are in the middle of the Atlantic, just past halfway between the U.S. and England, 1610 nautical miles from New York, 1591 nautical miles to Southampton, aboard the Queen Mary 2. So far it's an easy ride, south wind, sea is "slight" waves 1.5 to 4 ft. The sun is shining, doing its very best to make the billows smooth and bright. The sea is blue, blue somewhere between royal blue and indigo. The air temp is 71° F. The food is good and our cabin is nice. It's a slow trip but every day we enter a new time zone and I may not be keeping up with the QM2's 25 knots per hour.

Probably, because the euro is strong and the dollar is weak, and because the ship goes to Hamburg after leaving Southampton, the QM2 is full of Germans. They are mostly middle-aged, middle-class, I'd guess, or rich, returning home from a holiday in New York. The Germans, both sexes, are fond of wearing a kind of clam digger/cargo pant for casual dress. Casual dress is well planned. Germans do not just throw on a pair of jeans and a t-shirt. All the clothes look new. German men often wear leather shoes without socks, or sandals with socks. The English seem to be less fussy about their hair than the Germans. The Germans do German things the English do English things. Besides Germans, English and Americans there is a scattering of other nationalities: French, Spanish, Indian…. Between 3:30 and 4:30 PM the English have tea with little white bread sandwiches with the crusts cut off, tomato or cucumber and watercress, and sweets, cream scones with jam. I go to tea every day and pass as English because I really like those little sandwiches with the crusts cut off.

August 21. After retrieving our luggage we taxi to our hotel. Sounds kind of cool to say "… my hotel in London." We pass Big Ben. So now I have seen Big Ben, but I did not hear Big Ben bong. Our hotel in London is small, dumpy and very expensive. London is expensive, everyone says so, and I believe it. After we drop off our stuff we hike to Westminster Abby. Very impressive from the outside, but closed. Closed at 3:30. It is now 3:35. Keats, Blake, and all those other poets, not talking to me. "You got here too late, buster." So we have a bad pub lunch instead, at the Rochester. As we are finishing our soggy, overcooked vegetables three very tough looking young guys come in and order lunch. They look like football hoodlums to me, shaved heads, tattoos, big boots. But they are very polite hoodlums, and they each have two glasses of milk with their lunches.

August 25. We are on the ferry From Harwich, England to Hook of Holland, out in the open air on the top deck along with our new friends Jacqueline and Hans. Hans lives in Amsterdam and works for an institute that studies the causes of war. It is specialized work he says. He is also at work on a PhD in this subject. Jacqueline lives in Utrecht and is the director of three choirs. I gather that Hans and Jacqueline have been an item for a long time and often travel together. And they seem to have been everywhere, either together or separately. Jacqueline has hiked to the base camp of Mt. Everest. Hans has climbed Kilimanjaro. Hans has been to Australia. Jacqueline has ridden the Trans-Siberian train, from Moscow to Vladivostok. All of this, I gather, on a very small budget, lots of hiking and bicycling and "Fawlty Towers" hotels.

So I ask Hans, "What is it then, in a nutshell, what causes war?" "It's complicated," Hans says, "but it boils down to this, *everyone wants more*. Here in Europe though, after two world wars, we are pretty much done with war. We have learned it doesn't work. It's mostly a third world thing. Of course, the U.S. still starts wars when they have an interest, oil or something."

As the afternoon wears on Hans and I go to one of the bars on board and spend my remaining pounds sterling on beer. We talk about this and that. Hans says, "I was a juvenile delinquent, but when they were about to put me in jail I changed my ways. I really wanted to be a Mafia boss." "Don't you have to be Italian for that?" Hans is very fair and blonde. "It helps, I guess ... I have to finish this PhD because I've put so much into it, but when it's done I'm on to something else. This really isn't my kind of thing."

We are nearing Holland and I ask about the dikes. Hans says they pile up sand. "No," Jacqueline says, "it's peat." We discuss Hans Brinker. Was he the boy who put his finger in the dike? "No, no—silver skates." "Didn't he get silver skates for putting his finger in the dike?" No one knows.

After we disembark we meet with Hans and Jacqueline for a special treat: raw herring. Hans says it's fresh. Everybody waits for the fresh herring. We are at a little hot dog stand kind of place and, sure enough, people are lined up to get the fresh herring. It isn't entirely raw, I think, perhaps marinated briefly in something, but it's pink, and delicious, served with raw onions and bread. Ann is a bit hesitant.

We have decided, after talking with Hans and Jacqueline, to take the train to Delft for the night. We are all Vermeer fans and H & J say Delft is lovely. They show us to our train and we all say, "Goodbye, goodbye, what a pleasure it was ..."

After a few glasses of wine and a marvelous veal artichoke stew I am quite happy. We are sitting at an outdoor café in Delft watching the bicycles pass silently by on the other side of the canal. It is dusk and a young guy pedals by with his girl riding sidesaddle on the back.

There are bicycles everywhere, bicycles being ridden and bicycles parked in bicycle parking lots, hundreds and hundreds. Some look as though they have been parked for twenty or thirty, maybe fifty years.

September 4. *"So great, also, was the ornamentation of the ships, that the eyes of the beholders were dazzled, and to those looking from afar they seemed of flame rather than of wood. For if at any time the sun cast the splendor of its rays among them, the flashing of arms shone in one place, in another the flame of suspended shields. Gold shone on the prows, silver also flashed on the variously shaped ships. So great, in fact, was the magnificence of the fleet, that if its lord [Cnut] had desired to conquer any people, the ships alone would have terrified the enemy, before the warriors whom they carried joined battle at all. For who could look upon the lions of the foe, terrible with the brightness of gold, who upon the men of metal, menacing with golden face, who upon the dragons burning with pure gold, who upon the bulls on the ships threatening death, their horns shining with gold, without feeling any fear for the king of such a force?"*

Encomium Emmae Reginae (circa 1041)

Today we are viewing the Viking ships. The Oseberg ship and the Gokstad ship that were found in burial mounds in Vestfold county, Norway, beautiful and beautifully preserved ships from the 8th or 9th century.

Because Viking ships did not have a deep keel and had a fair amount of freeboard, they tended to slip sideways in the water, whether under sail or not. This is known as leeway, the ship slips sideways into the lee of the wind. So even with the most skilled sailors it was easy to get blown off course.

Perhaps this is what happened to Sven Torfyndr (Sven the Hard to Find). Sven was hard to find because he spent a great deal of time at sea. Part of the reason for that was Sven's wife Hildur Big Nose. It was the practice in those times to nickname people, and often the nickname referred to a prominent and unflattering physical feature or habit. Hildur Big Nose, to distinguish her from Hildur the Short. Hakan Hairy Legs, son of Erik, to distinguish him from the other Hakans, sons of other Eriks. Hakan Erikson. It is a confusion that still goes on. Someone once asked me if I knew the Johnsons in Duluth.

Sven was throwing a little fish boil down at the dock and seriously entertaining Arnbjörg Long Legs. It was a beautiful evening, near mid summer, a lingering twilight. Sven and Arnbjörg were tossing back a few tankards of mead and having some laughs when Hildur came along and crashed the party, began screaming at Sven, pulled Arnbjörg's hair, kicked over the cooking tripod nearly setting fire to Sven's ship, the "Wave Pounder," and spilling the fish stew. Sven knew then that it was time to go back to sea.

September 5. I am walking the streets of Oslo with my friend Dag who is from Trondheim. We are on the way to meet his brother Kjell who works at a newspaper. We are talking about poems and poets we like, and before we know it we are lost. Dag doesn't know Oslo any better than I do, so he asks directions from a guy working on the street. He answers our questions in a mix of Norwegian and English. I think he thinks we are both Americans. After we are on our way again Dag says "That guy was from the north. He had a northern accent." Dag says there is still a prejudice against northerners in Oslo, that northerners are thought of as hicks, barbarians. He says in the 1950s, you might see an ad in the newspaper that read "Apartment for rent: No smokers, no drinkers, no people from the north."

Every few blocks in Oslo there is a bad accordion player, someone from Bulgaria or Romania probably, trying to make a few kroner, his hat in front of him with a few coins as bait. The music is so bad that you would happily pay to have them stop playing. The players seem to appear at regular intervals. I think this must be a franchise operation. One rents the accordion, is given some rudimentary lessons, then is assigned a territory and pays regular rent on that space.

September 7. The pay toilet in the Oslo central railway station is quite complex, very nearly as complicated as the security system at the Munch Museum, which is every bit as complex as airport security. Well, "The Scream" was stolen, so the media (I am told) cried out for more security and they got it. Now they are crying that the security is too much. The theft of "The Scream" was merely a ploy, an attempt to divert police attention (I am also told) away from a series of bank robberies. Anyway, the "toallet" in the Oslo train station is quite secure. It is equipped with a change machine, gates, which will open only after one has deposited 10 kroner, and a man in a kind of ticket booth to make sure that no one tries to slip in without paying, no matter how distressed that person may be. Pay public toilets are common in Norway, I think. I don't know if this is a state run operation like the liquor stores, or if this is an entrepreneurial activity. Perhaps someone owns a chain of pay toilets, kind of like a chain of car washes. Perhaps, someone now serving in parliament made his fortune in the toilet business.

September 10. We have met our friends Ann and Herb in Kalmar, Sweden. We all have Swedish ancestors and we are looking around at various towns and villages where they lived. Ann is a connoisseur of "cute," cute houses, cute villages ... This leads to a discussion of what constitutes cute. I ask Ann what makes something cute?

"I'm not sure 'cute' exists in nature. A cute valley maybe, or a little town with a bridge, if it's small and sheltering, but a mountain or forest? Uh uh. It's definitely different than beautiful. And cute can't be cloying. I think Disneyland is just annoying. Cute is little, like a little table in a bay window with a geranium in a pot, or a little pond instead of a big lake, or a little study as opposed to a big living room. And cute is little in people too. Tall people aren't cute, little people with curly hair and long eyelashes and dimples are cute." But then, I thought, isn't that a matter of perspective? To a twenty-foot tall troll, would a six-foot tall human be cute?

We agree that true cute has to be authentic, not manufactured like ET or Hummel figurines. Real cute is not sentimental, but our reaction to it may be. We agree also that Europe is cuter than the U.S. "Which is cuter," I ask Ann, "Sweden or Switzerland?" She says, 'I think now I vote for Switzerland. It's more sheltered. Like having a blanket around you. Little balconies on chalets, little built-in cupboards ...'"

Later I asked my friend Richard about cute. He said, "I never considered cute as a concept but it must exist somewhere along the spectrum between the sublime and the ridiculous."

September 21. We are leaving Trondheim, where we have spent some very nice days with poets and friends, for Åndalsnes, then by rental car to Ålesund where we hope to meet the Norwegian painter Ørnulf Opdahl. Then we will go on to Copenhagen, Amsterdam, across the channel again to Harwich, and on to Halesworth, Suffolk, UK.

Of the 10,000 things that one has to deal with daily, I could, in the past, manage about 6537 of them. Nowadays my numbers are down to 2724 and falling. But on the train, like this, the 10,000 things pass by my window and disappear.

Trees and cows and hedges and bridges, rivers, canals and boats, people and dogs, horses, cars waiting at the crossing as we whiz past, clouds and sky, minivans, suddenly a train passing in the opposite direction at 100 mph… whoosh, and the whole train shudders, apple trees, a nuclear power plant. There are mountains in the distance that suddenly appear right in front of you, long tunnels where everything goes black and when you emerge once more into the light, the train has turned 180 degrees, and far below are waterfalls and tiny farms and miniscule sheep lying down in green pastures.

Pipelines, power lines, rusting track, barbed wire, brickyards, broken glass, paper cups, beer bottles … huge impossible, unnamable constructions of concrete, steel and pigeon shit all being demolished to sell to the Chinese to make hair dryers and toasters. It is the hapless, hopeless backside of the city you see as you arrive by train. And people live there right by the tracks.

My wife does not like to ride facing the back of the train, but sometimes those are the only available seats. Today the train is full, people talking on their mobile phones, all over Europe people on trains talking on their mobiles in a dozen different languages and they are all saying, "I'm on the train." It doesn't bother me usually, going backwards, but I guess in a way it is like life, one has no inkling of what is ahead, the future, only a blurred sideways glimpse of the present, and the immediate past quickly receding into the mist. When I think of it like that, I don't much care for it either.

But still, I like riding the train, particularly if I can ride first class. It is seldom crowded and the seats are comfortable. I can lean back and watch the whole plotless, pointless movie play out on my big screen train window.

September 28. Dean, a poet and a very funny guy, and one of the employees of the Poetry Trust, (the people who invited me to England), drives us to Norwich. Dean says, "I want you to listen to this broad Norfolk accent you hear in Norwich." "What?" I say, "Norwich is only thirty miles away!" But thirty miles is a long way in England. The road twists and turns, stops and starts, winds through towns and villages and roundabouts ... and everyone drives on the wrong side of the road.

October 1. Much of our time in England we stay at the Corner House in Aldeburgh, our hosts Richard and Pippa are most gracious, the food is excellent and the company splendid. Aldeburgh is on the Suffolk coast and is famous as the onetime home of Benjamin Britten and the music festival he founded. Aldeburgh is the home also of the Aldeburgh Poetry Festival, one of the events in which I have been invited to participate. But perhaps Aldeburgh's greatest claim to fame is that it is home to "England's best fish and chips."

October 5. One evening Ann and I take a walk on the beach and stop to chat with a local fisherman who is selling his catch at one of the little shacks along the shore. Most of the shacks are closed. I asked how he fished? "Long lines, nets, pots ... but the North Sea is fished out. There is pollution, global warming. There are too many people." "On that cheerful note ..." I say. He laughs, "Enjoy the day," he says.

October 9. On the train from Bath to Swansea we meet a young man of Iranian descent who was raised in Paris. He is on his way to do post graduate work at the University of Wales, some kind of engineering. I ask if he goes to Iran often? "Yes I still have family there. It is strange, in a way I feel connected to Iran but it is not home and neither is France, really. I want to think of myself as a world citizen. There is too much nationalism. It only causes problems." I agree. Later I ask if he follows football. "Oh, yes." "What team do you root for?" "Usually León ..." he pauses a moment, "but really, I root for anyone against England."

October 11. In all of Wales' green valleys there are sheep, it seems, and the sheep all look as though they have been spray-painted. Some have red marks on their backs and some have blue. *Is this a way of branding?* I wonder. But here are red marked sheep in one field and red marked sheep in the next field. How would one know the difference? I turns out that the most common reason for the color is from a marking device strapped to a ram's chest.

Raddle—coloured pigment used to mark sheep for various reasons, such as to show ownership, or to show which lambs belong to which ewe. May be strapped to the chest of a ram, to mark the backs of ewes he mates (different rams may be given different colours). Also a verb ("that ewe's been raddled"). Also "ruddy." ("Sheep husbandry," from Wikipedia, the free encyclopedia.)

So it's a way seeing which sheep may be pregnant and to check up on the old boy to make sure he is doing his job. It's the red ram versus the blue ram. Which causes me to wonder if there are any purple markings out there, or maroon? Are there red or blue markings on anything other than ewes? Do yellow or green markings appear mysteriously? What happens to a ram if he doesn't make enough marks? If he gets too old and tired? Does he become mutton or a hat rack?

October 14. We are at Harlech Castle, located in Harlech, Gwynedd, Wales. Harlech is a concentric castle, constructed atop a cliff, 200 feet above the Irish Sea. The castle was built by King Edward I during his conquest of Wales in 1283. The close proximity to sea allowed for a quick escape when the Welsh besieged the castle. It must have been a cold, lonely outpost. "Go home Edward!" the Welsh are saying. The troops are gone now and even the sea has gone, retreated several miles from the castle. The castle is a fine tourist attraction and the sea floor is now a golf course:

"Dress should be not less than "*smart casual*" both on the course and in the Clubhouse, and this does not include such items as jeans, tee shirts, football shirts and training wear. Tailored shorts are permitted on the course with long stockings or short white socks and in the Clubhouse up until 6.00 p.m."

October 20. The weather in Sligo is "soft," as an Irish friend of mine says. "When it isn't actually pouring rain but just drizzling, gray and foggy, it's called soft." The weather is bad. I stand on Hyde Bridge and look down into the river. There is a red umbrella swirling around upside down in a back eddy along with the other debris, beer cans, cigarette butts, sticks and paper. I wonder if this weather finally got to someone, probably a woman, since the umbrella is red, and she leapt into the Garavogue.

Today Bare Ben Bulben's head is covered by a layer of cloud. We wander on downtown where there is a statue of Mr. Yeats looking very disdainful, very snooty, I think. Probably looking at me and saying "Prose poem?"

Later in the afternoon we visit into a pub we like and have a Guinness. Guinness beer in Ireland is unlike Guinness beer anywhere else. I never liked the stuff I got in the US. But in Ireland I tasted and it was an epiphany. I understood. I understood why in the morning, outside any given pub, anywhere in Ireland, there are 50 to 100 empty kegs waiting to be replaced by full kegs, and the Guinness truck was there: ask and ye shall receive.

I ask the bartender about traditional music in Sligo. She says, "I don't know. I like all kinds of music, jazz, classical, rock … but I can't stand that whack-fol-the-diddle stuff.

October 21. It is difficult to get from Sligo to Drumcliff churchyard where William Yeats is laid unless you have an automobile. It is a long and expensive taxi ride. The bus will drop you there but that means you are there for the day, until the bus returns in the evening. We decide just to wave from the window on our way to Donegal, busman pass by.

October 26. London. We have visited so many art museums in New York, London, Dublin, Oslo, wandered through room after room, looked at so much that I get lost and confused. "Didn't I see that Kandinsky just a few minutes ago?" And so many people; today I saw Picasso himself, among the Picassos of course, short, stocky, bald, wearing Bermuda shorts, as usual but, because he was in a museum I suppose, today wearing a pink polo shirt.

November 8. Dartmoor is an area of moorland in the centre of Devon, England. Protected by National Park status, it covers 368 square miles in the southwest of England. Our friends Peter and Mimi (whom we have not seen in 30 years) live in the nearby town of Buckfastleigh. The morning after an evening of catching up on things and a goodly portion of good Scotch, Peter takes us on a tour of the moor. It is a lonely, wild place and it is gray November, damp and windy. We hike a ways near the River Dart and up on the moor.

There are wild moor ponies scratching themselves on the big stone menhirs, or standing stones, which date back to the late Neolithic age. Nobody really knows what purpose these stones served, but Peter says it is a good idea to hug one, so we hug one. In addition to the standing stones there are stone circles, kistvaens, cairns and stone rows, and the names of the stones and the places are wonderful: Beardown Man, near Devil's Tor, Challacombe, near the prehistoric settlement of Grimspound, Drizzlecombe, east of Sheepstor village, Grey Wethers, near Postbridge, Scorhill, west of Chagford.

The moor is vast and mostly treeless. It is a place of legend. Dartmoor was said to have been visited by the Devil during the Great Thunderstorm of 1638. It is the setting for *The Hound of the Baskervilles*, and in more recent times there is the story of The Hairy Hands that takes place on a stretch of road in Dartmoor between Postbridge and Two Bridges, Dartmoor. The road is now known as the B3212, which was purported to have seen an unusually high number of motor vehicle accidents during the early 20th century.

According to the story the Hairy Hands are a pair of disembodied hands that appear suddenly, grab at the steering wheel of a moving car or the handlebars of a motorcycle, and then force the victim off the road. Journalist and author Rufus Endle claimed that, while driving near Postbridge "a pair of hands gripped the driving wheel and I had to fight for control." He managed to avoid a crash and the hands disappeared as inexplicably as they had come. Other victims were less fortunate than

Rufus Endle, and met their untimely deaths on the lonely moor road because of THE HAIRY HANDS.

As we watch from a hill, a procession of ten or twelve people wind their way, single file, across the moor, men and women, I think, but it is difficult to tell at this distance, and each of these people is carrying a long wooden pole. They do not see us, or they ignore us as they walk away into the mist, The weather is getting worse. It's time to get out of here.

November 13. In France there is a lot of dog shit. One notices the beautiful architecture of Nice, the enchanting blue Mediterranean, the markets, the fashion, but one also notices, or had better notice, that the sidewalks are covered with dog shit. People love their dogs here. There are, as you might expect, a lot of poodles, little Fifi poodles and big standard poodles but there are also rottweilers with muzzles and little mop-like dogs, dogs of all sorts actually, and their owners make no attempt to clean up after them.

So we are stepping carefully around Nice and the sky is blue and the sea is blue. It is cool but not cold. We are staying at the hotel L'Oasis where Chekhov once stayed while trying to recover from tuberculosis. He rewrote part of *Three Sisters* here. The hotel is modest and inexpensive by Nice standards and no doubt much changed from Chekhov's day. Still I can imagine him in his suit and pince-nez reading in the garden. Chekhov said that Nice was a good place to read but not to write. On the telephone I tell my brother-in-law that we are staying in Chekhov's hotel. He tells me that he once stayed in the same hotel room that Werner Heisenberg had occupied back in 1926. He thought it was either in Copenhagen or Leipzig, but he was uncertain.

November 27. We have been to Lucca, Parma, Florence, Milan and in two days we will be on our way home aboard the Costa Mediterannea. During most of our time in Italy the weather has been gray damp and chilly. Well, it is November. Back home deer season is just over, Thanksgiving is over and there is Christmas crap everywhere. It is gray and cold and gloomy. I find that I am writing about November again. It is more a state of mind than a month. But to write about November is like writing another song about Indiana, a state that has more songs written about it than the state itself merits. Today there is a mistral here in Savona. The sky is bright and the wind is cold.

Words and Pictures

2012

MAGNUM OPUS

Back then, I wrote all the time, I wrote like a madman, and I was, of course, alone in my dingy little apartment with the nearby freight trains rattling the windows all night long, accentuating my loneliness. It was love, unrequited passion. Nowadays, my ardor cooled somewhat by the years, I write down lines on little scraps of paper and if I come across them, weeks or months, maybe even years later, (the way time goes) they may become part of the magnum opus, or maybe not. I can foresee the time when I will cease to bother with paper and pencils, a more eco-friendly method, and just formulate and arrange the words in my head, and then, later maybe, not even that. Perhaps then the thoughts, the unformed notions will arrive and pass by like birds or wisps of clouds, leaving the sky clear and blue.

OLD WIRING

It is ridiculous to worry about the next world when you can't even do much about this one. I worry about global climate change, about Yellowstone exploding, cosmic debris hitting the earth. I have worried about nuclear weapons in Iran and North Korea until I was just about to doze off. But there is something else, something else ... some darkness lurking always nearby ... Then I remember that tangle of wiring in the attic that dates back to the nineteen-twenties, a potential fire-hazard, for sure. I should hire an electrician, but that would be so expensive ... I think I'll just let the nameless dread roost there for a while in that nest of wires, while I go for a whiskey, down at the old Knob and Tube.

BUCKET OF BOLTS

My grandpa had the first car in town, a 1904 Auburn. When the car developed engine trouble and stopped running there was no one in town who could fix it. So they pushed the car into the blacksmith shop and carefully removed the engine and put each bolt they removed into a bucket. Then they crated up the engine and shipped it, by train, back to the manufacturer in Indiana. In a few weeks the crate came back with a note that the engine had been repaired at no cost to the owner. The problem now was that no one could remember how to put the engine back in the car. There was much discussion, everyone had a theory; the barber, the druggist, even the minister had a few thoughts. Finally the project had to be abandoned. The car never ran again but the engine sat in its crate in the blacksmith shop for years. People went on to other things, births, deaths, new cars ... But a thing like that can persist beyond a lifetime, or two, beyond any memory of its existence, lying in a field somewhere with weeds growing up around it. You could stumble over it if you aren't careful.

Tin Flag

2013

BASEMENT

There's something about our basement that causes forgetting. I go down for something, say a roll of paper towels, which we keep in a big box down there, and as soon as I get to the bottom of the stairs I have forgotten what I came down there for. It happens to my wife as well. So recently we have taken to working in tandem like spelunkers. One of us stands at the top of the stairs while the other descends. When the descendant has reached the bottom stair, the person at the top calls out, "Light bulbs, 60 watt." This usually works unless the one in the basement lingers too long. I blame this memory loss on all the stuff in the basement. Too much baggage: 10 shades of blue paint, because we could not get the right color, extra dishes, bicycles, the washer and dryer, a cider press, a piano, jars of screws, nails and bolts ... It boggles the mind. My wife blames it on radon.

SIT DOWN

I often spend a good portion of each day trying to find the right place to sit down. The place you choose to sit must be the right height, not too low because of the difficulty of rising again. An Adirondack chair is a bad choice, as is a canoe. I know of two or three rocks along the shore of Lake Superior that I find to be of a comfortable height and good for a short stay; hardness is another factor. Sofas are usually a bad choice, especially if it's your girlfriend's parent's sofa. Don't sit on the edge of a bed. Chairs in the dentist's office waiting room are always uncomfortable. Actually, an overturned bucket overlooking a hole in the ice is probably better, but not by much.

On a sunny day in late March or early April you can get yourself a good sturdy straight-backed chair and go to the south side of the shack, sit down and lean back, chair and all, against the sun-warmed tarpaper wall. You've got the back legs of the chair planted in the snow for extra support. You can just doze there, while the sunlight soaks into the black paper-covered wall, and into you, and you soak into the black background, deeper and deeper until you disappear.

LIFE IN THE WOODS

The woods around you have grown up sheerly to depress you with their dampness and dark. The small birds have all flown away, leaving you alone in the gloom. For a point of reference there's a pile of rusted cans and broken bottles. For company there are mosquitoes. If you call out for help you are put on hold.

If you live long enough in the forest, the forest people, some so old and bent over that their long noses touch the ground, the hidden ones, those conversant with the moon and the devil and the west wind, may come in the night once or twice a month and clean your bathroom. Or not. Which means they don't like you.

HAIRCUT

Shall I wait to get my haircut after my hair has gotten too long, have it cut too short and await the day, the hour, when my hair reaches its perfect length? Or should I have it cut often, keeping my coif constantly at its optimum length? That becomes expensive and besides I like to live in anticipation of the moment. But the moment passes so quickly. For instance, there must have been a period in my life when I was at my peak. Maybe it was only a year or so when, at last, I got my act together, maybe for only a few weeks, or days, when my mental and physical powers were at their fullest. Maybe it was only a couple of hours in the early morning of some forgotten day and I slept through the whole thing. And when I woke, things had begun to deteriorate.

AWAKE AT NIGHT

They lie awake for an hour or more, motionless, neither speaking, under their covers making a shape like two low hills or like two long gray clouds that roll in on an afternoon in late fall. Perhaps they will lie like this, side by side, after death, silent until she says, "What time is it?" And he says, "2093."

Maybe she wants to talk. She says, "I'm having a lot of trouble with Photoshop." And he says, "I don't want to talk about software right now." She snuggles close and says, "Do you want to talk about hardware then?"

STARRY STARRY NIGHT

A bazillion stars overhead, and I look up as amazed and baffled as the first hominid who gazed upward must have been, stars passing overhead like a very slow moving flock of birds, going somewhere, disappearing into the wee hours of the morning. I used to be able to recognize some of the constellations, the Pleiades, the Big Dipper, but I have forgotten most. Still, mankind has learned a lot about the cosmos since Galileo's time. A friend of mine said, "My wife bought me a telescope for my birthday, a nice one, very powerful, I've got it set up on the deck. You know, when you look at a star with your naked eye all you see is a little white dot, but when you look at it through a telescope you see a bigger white dot."

THE PERSONAL HISTORY CHANNEL

For a few dollars more a month you can add the Personal History Channel to your cable package. You can then while away the hours, reviewing the stupid and embarrassing things you did in years gone by. It can be fascinating watching yourself learning to ride a bicycle or going on your first date. When you come to more recent times, however, there are more and more shows that feature you sitting on the couch, eating chips and watching the Personal History Channel.

IN LESS THAN TEN MINUTES

You have to loosen a bolt that's stuck and does not want to budge, God knows why. It was torqued to specs with the finest tools. It is a very delicate operation, the bolt must not be broken. In order to do this you have to work standing on your head. And because of that your white tie drops down into your spaghetti sauce and you break a button that holds up your pants and in less than ten minutes the King of Bhutan is going to present you with an award. Well, you can tie up your pants with the cord that you wear around your neck that holds your ID card, which will then dangle between your legs, and you can paint your tie with more sauce so that it will appear that you have very bad taste, rather than being merely clumsy.... This is the kind of thing we like to do.

RASPBERRY RHUBARB PIE

Ann has just taken one of her famous pies from the oven, and the crust has separated all around the perimeter so that the hot filling bubbles up, like lava from a Hawaiian volcano. It is very hot. The crust of the pie floats on the hot filling the way the earth's surface floats on its core of molten magma. Perhaps the center of the earth is hot raspberry-rhubarb filling, but you can't have any, it is much too hot. You are going to have to wait a very long time before you can have any.

SANDALS

I never really feel comfortable wearing sandals. They don't seem right for this northern climate. Up here we are always expecting it to turn cold. We never go anywhere without a jacket. So when it gets warm enough to wear sandals, usually four or five days in early August, it feels as though I'm taking a big risk to do so. Sandals make me realize how vulnerable I am, nothing at all to protect my toes from falling rocks or scalding hot water. If you wear sandals your feet are available to mosquitoes and wood ticks and other vermin. You don't want to walk into the woods wearing sandals; you don't want to play soccer or rugby. I feel more at ease in boots and wool socks, but every summer I wear my sandals once or twice as an indicator that I'm not planning to do anything at all.

REGRET

There's no use in regret. You can't change anything. Your mother died unhappy with the way you turned out. You and your father were not on speaking terms when he died, and you left your wife for no good reason. Well, it's past. You may as well regret missing out on the conquest of Mexico. That would have been just your kind of thing back when you were eighteen: a bunch of murderous Spaniards, out to destroy a culture and get rich. On the other hand, the Aztecs were no great shakes either. It's hard to know whom to root for in this situation. The Aztecs thought they had to sacrifice lots of people to keep the sun coming up every day. And it worked. The sun rose every day. But it was backbreaking labor, all that sacrificing. The priests had to call in the royal family to help, and their neighbors, the gardener, the cooks ... You can see how this is going to end. You are going to have your bloody, beating heart ripped out, but you are going to have to stand in line, in the hot sun, for hours, waiting your turn.

ZUCCHINI

You always miss one, and the one overlooked, hidden behind one of the large leaves, grows to an enormous size. These things are best when they are small. You can't give this monster away. You say, "It will make great zucchini bread." "Hmmm, no thanks." What to do? Here you are, responsible for an overweight vegetable. This is not what you had in mind when you planted the seeds. But you can't just throw it away. It looks like you will have to make zucchini bread, even though you don't much like zucchini bread. Perhaps you could give away the zucchini bread after you've made it. On the other hand, you could put the zucchini into a nice basket, along with some carrots and onions or some flowers, place it on someone's porch, ring the door bell and run away.

TANGO

In a relationship like this there is one who does not really care, and that forces the other into the position of the one who does: positive and negative forces, so that things will go around. A tango. The long summer evening, the music ... "Why do you treat me this way?" she asks. "I love you, of course ..." "I hate you," she says. He takes her hand and pulls her close. "Be careful ... my husband ... He has a pistol." He doesn't. She made that up. They are careful of the steps, the turns. It is complicated and they are intense, breathless ... the other dancers close by. But it is night that is important, the breeze is warm in the beckoning aspen grove where there are lovely grassy clearings. The stars are appearing one by one, and the moon is a mere beginning over the lake, a sliver in the indigo sky.

When the music ends he says, "Thank you, my dear." And she says, "Oh no, thank you!"

EXERCISE

Here is a Zen-inspired exercise for all you older guys. Dress comfortably in your shorts and a tee-shirt, hold your trousers in front of you with both hands. You will need to bend forward somewhat in order to hold your pants at knee level or below. Then while balancing on your right leg, lift your left leg and insert it into the left pant leg. Repeat this process lifting your right and balancing on your left leg. See if you can do this without tipping over. Practice without using a chair or other support. This exercise is best done quickly and without thought. But, of course, now you have thought about it.

CONFUSING FALL WARBLERS

This is the way things go: not high and direct like the geese with all their honking fanfare, or the eagle riding the rising air, but like the small birds feeding, moving from bush to tree to weed, with what seems like no plan at all, just one thing leading to another.

STORIES YOU TELL

There are worse things than being a human being, I suppose. You could be a politician, for instance. The only compensation for being human is that you can make up a good story. But good stories require a good audience, one that is patient and quiet. You could try telling a story to a cow. You'd want to gear the story to your audience. "Once upon a time I walked over by the fence and I stood there for a long time, chewing, looking out across the road ... then suddenly PLOP, I dropped a big cow pie. Ha ha ha ha!" The cow just stares at you, chewing. It's no good with dogs either, dogs listen, often with great enthusiasm, but they don't really get it. No good with cats or monkeys. That means you are pretty much stuck with other human beings as your audience. You spend a lifetime getting the stories just right and then you begin: "Once upon a time I walked over by the fence ..." and the listener stares into space, chewing, wondering vaguely how long this will last.

BREAKFAST

Now that the fun is over maybe it is time to take yourself away to a hermitage high in the mountains, to become a contemplative. But one doesn't want to rush into something like that. It's difficult. Once we stayed out all night drinking under the summer stars and at two a.m. someone said, "Let's drive to Aspen." "Great idea!" We don't do that anymore. What's left then? I think, breakfast. Perhaps a bowl of oatmeal, with raisins, or a soft-boiled egg …The sun is shining; a touch of fall in the air, and coffee is ready. The other morning some old friends called, people I haven't seen in fifty years, people with whom I have nothing in common. "We just got married! We're in town, on our honeymoon!" Ridiculous. "Well hell," I said. "Come on over, we'll have some coffee, some bacon and eggs. We'll talk about protein and carbohydrates. We'll talk about distance and speed and gas mileage."

In the Sun
Out of the Wind

2017

BLACK BEARS

I like black bears. They are relatively common around here, and they are usually not aggressive. Actually, they are generally affable, loners mostly, but not opposed to hanging out with humans now and then. In fact, I've found that in many ways they are a lot like us.

My friend, Richard, an older male, drops by now and then and we hang out down on the shore, have a couple of beers, but mostly we just sit and look out at the water. We don't have a lot to say. We aren't friends exactly, but we enjoy the company. Richard says, at our age we don't have friends. We have associates.

WHY?

I ask myself. Because when you finally need to go home this is the only place to go to. And when you get there there's nothing; just the blank page. Well, maybe there's a patch of dry bare ground, underneath an old cottonwood tree, a bit of sun, a crow in the next field. You can add things or take them away. Youth was the age of acquisition. Now you find that there aren't many things you need, but the garage and the attic are still full. I'm OK with the dirt and the cottonwood tree. It's not the bodhi tree, but my expectations are not high. The oceans are deep and dark and the briny water goes on for thousands of miles, but you only need a cupful or so to drown in.

THE WOODS IN FALL

In the city it seems no one treats you as a human being. The woods, on the other hand, are full of things that do, that run if you come too close. It's lonely. Who will I talk to? Who will I invite to my birthday party? Bears tend to overindulge and fall asleep. Alfred, the great gray owl, commonly known as Al Owl, can never remember anyone's name.... The days are bright and the nights clear and cold. Most all the leaves have fallen by now, the red and orange maple, the yellow birch and poplar. Only the somber evergreens are unmoved. If I clear a few of the dead leaves from this little pool there is the perfect sky again, on the other side, and a face, not quite mine, but that apes my every move and refuses to go away until I do.

AFTER MIDNIGHT

After midnight Woodland Avenue is quiet for the most part, an occasional car and then a motorcycle winding up, going way too fast. Someone drunk with love or the lack thereof, drunk with speed, with despair or joie de vivre, someone young and immortal, stalking death. "Live fast, love hard, die young and leave a beautiful memory." But memory is short, not much more than the day after tomorrow. So go ahead then I say, take some innocent bystanders with you—passion is over in an eyeblink, whether you die or live.

CROWS BEHIND THE HOUSE

Crows have gathered in the trees behind the house, cawing and carrying on all afternoon. They are upset about something. We have been told how smart crows are, how they can recognize individual human faces, how they can learn to use tools, how they can communicate. Which is great, except that they hardly ever shut up. Crows are very intelligent, perhaps as smart or smarter than monkeys or chimpanzees, which to my mind, given their ubiquity, puts them in strong contention for second most annoying species on the planet. Or maybe third, behind mosquitoes.

DUCKS

There are two types of ducks, divers and dabblers. Divers feed on fish, plants and insects in deep water. They live on big lakes and rivers. Dabblers prefer shallow water, ponds and creeks where they feed on plants and insects. Dabblers are also known as puddle ducks. Once, on a very rainy day, I saw a mallard land on water that had accumulated in the street, not more than 6 or 7 inches deep. If I decided to be a duck I'd probably choose to be a dabbler, it's more my nature, dabbling here and there, farting around, not like a diver, some sharp-billed merganser intent on something lurking in the deep. And unlike the diving ducks who need a long runway to become airborne, running and flapping along the surface of the water, dabblers take off from the water with a sudden, upward leap into the air.

UNTROUBLED

One wearies of matters of substance, those weighty matters that one feels should be resolved, the dilemma of life on earth, the existence of extra-terrestrial life, the existence of God. Instead I recommend those moments that, seemingly without reason, stay with you for a lifetime: that red-haired girl on the shore brushing her teeth as we sailed away; the glimpse of a face; a bare shoulder turning in a doorway; moments like music, beauty and truth untroubled by meaning.

HERE AND THERE

Some days I don't know if I'm coming or going, as they say. Don't know if I'm here or there. I am here and you are there. Except, of course, when you are here or I am there. I much prefer it when you are here. Then it seems that spring is truly on the way, that the sun is warming and the lilacs will bloom. But then sometimes I think that you are not really here, that there is a faraway look in your eyes, that in fact you are far away. I don't know where you are, London? New York? Maybe you are just outside the door, but you are there and I am still here.

SMILE

There is a beautiful young woman behind the counter and for no apparent reason she gives me a smile that is devastating. It is a smile that is like the sunlight coming through the heavy clouds and turning the surface of the water all glittery silver. It is a smile that says anything is possible, that I am the one she has been waiting for, that I am 25 again. I think she must be the most cruel person on the planet. She puts her hand under mine as she gives me my change, and all I can say is "Oh my heart."

NORTH SHORE

On a clear day like today I can see the Wisconsin shore all the way to Outer Island and miles of white-capped waves rising and falling between here and there. The rock I am sitting on is huge and round with a fringe of moss, like hair, around the edge just below the waterline. It is like sitting atop a monk's head. I reach down and the cold water surges up to touch my hand. It occurs to me that we are already under way and I have no idea how to pilot this thing.

BEAUTIFUL WOMEN

There are all these women, beautiful young women and they circle around you, no, not circle but they pass so close. They have things to do, places to go, they stride past you on the street in their skirts and high boots and you want to say wait, wait ... and one gives you a quick kiss as she passes by and you want to say wait ... but there is another ... and then they are all gone ... and they pass far away, like objects in the sky, like a satellite, like some blinking billionaire's jet plane, silent, high above, and down here on earth it's turning cold and it's late.

PUTTY FROM VASELINE

Did I tell you about the newlyweds who could not tell putty from Vaseline? Yes, my wife says, about a hundred times. That's the trouble, I say, you know every one of my stories and jokes, I need some new young woman to tell my stories to. You could try getting some new stories, my wife says. No, that's no good. I'm too old for that, all that stuff happened when I was young. What I need is a fresh ear, some beautiful young woman who would laugh and think that maybe my stories were even profound and she'd hug me and say, Let's go for a ski, and then go out dancing. And I'd say, Can't we just stay in this afternoon, make a fire ... ? Then she'd say, Come on, don't be an old fuddy-duddy. If you don't want to come along I'll go alone. Wait, I'd say. Did I tell you about the newlyweds ... ?

LOSS

It isn't so much because of the desire for what has been lost, as it is the loss of desire itself, that I stand here, like a child whose big rubber ball has washed out to sea, on the verge of tears, becoming aware that there is no possibility of return.

THE DREAMTIME

Those were the days of beer and deep-fried chicken livers, at night we swam the laughing sea. You were so beautiful. It was still the dreamtime, we were still in the aureole of childhood that extended a hundred thousand light years into deep space. But eventually even that ended and we fell into our separate realities. Everything fell apart. We all went crazy, they discovered water on Mars, the Nasdaq went down 3 percent, and suddenly we were too old. Yet it would be great to meet you at the Dreamtime Supper Club for one last dance, and a cocktail, perhaps.

BLUE SHIRT

I've gotten up many a morning in recent years, taken a look in the mirror and said, "Alright, it's got to be the life of the mind from here on out." But despite tremendous effort I found myself incapable of a single thought, and totally exhausted by 10:00 a.m. So looking good is important. Though in my case there is not much to work with, especially when I consider the ordinary mess of my life, the ragtag collection of mistakes and wrong turns, the worn out socks and underwear stored in a cardboard box. But I do have the blue shirt my wife bought for me. It is a beautiful dark blue, cut so that it hangs just right and made of a material that is comfortable in all seasons. Even though it doesn't make up for anything, and no one ever notices, I always feel good when I wear it.

LUCKY

All my life I've been lucky. Not that I made money, or had a beautiful house or cars. But lucky to have had good friends, a wife who loves me, and a good son. Lucky that war and famine or disease did not come to my doorstep. Lucky that all the wrong turns I made, even if they did not turn out well, at least were not complete disasters. I still have some of my original teeth. All that could change, I know, in the wink of an eye. And what an eye it is, bright blue contrasting with her dark skin and black hair. And oh, what long eyelashes! She turns and with a slight smile gives me a long slow wink, a wink that says, "Come on over here, you lucky boy."

INHERITANCE

My father came from nowhere in particular, and he was only distantly related to anyone, second cousin once removed. He came wearing a white suit, slammed into the hog pen when the brakes failed. The only things he owned were a few tools. He rose early. He went up and down the ladder, painting maroon or chartreuse, round and round the room in a sort of dance. He painted his face in a random pattern. Round and round till he fell down flat. I don't own the tools but I know some of the steps, some of the words to the song.

GOING THROUGH A PHASE

My granddaughter, age two, lies on the floor and kicks and screams and cries, Mommy, Daddy! I need help! she sobs. It is a moment of existential angst. I know exactly what she means. She's going through a phase, they say. That's how life is, one phase after another. I remember the phase of thinking I was Elvis, even though I couldn't sing. And in junior high there was the phase of being "mentally challenged." I hung out all summer with the dumbest kid in school. We rode our bicycles aimlessly around town and one day on a quiet street I rode straight into the back of a parked car. Probably because of that incident, I have never fully recovered from that phase. In fact, in recent years I've detected a resurgence of the condition.

LEOTI

Great Grandpa Charlie thought he could get rich in America so he came to Leoti, Kansas in the 1870s. There was a fight going on over which town, Leoti or nearby Coronado, would be the county seat. Wyatt Earp and Bat Masterson came to help shoot it out. Everybody felt there was money to be made. At this time, also, they were killing off the buffalo. Charlie got a wagon and he gathered the bones of slaughtered buffalo to sell to be made into fertilizer, and the horns were made into buttons. By the time the bones were all gone he'd made enough to buy some land, get married and build a sod house. Great Grandpa didn't stay too many years. It was a difficult place to farm, flat and hard as a gaming table, treeless and dusty. Leoti won the war and is still county seat and the only town in the county. After the fight everyone moved out of Coronado. At the courthouse we located Great Grandpa's settlement on the big county map. My wife said, "We could drive out there and have a picnic." The clerk said, "I wouldn't do that if I were you. They raise a lot of pigs out there nowadays."

HERITAGE

Great-Grandmother Murphy was a proud woman. She came from a well-to-do family that had connections back east. She had presence and bearing. Great-Grandpa Murphy was an Irishman of dubious ancestry and background. Nevertheless they got married, as people do. Grandpa Murphy shuffled along as they walked downtown, looking at the ground or his feet. He found things that way; an Indian arrowhead, sometimes a nickel or a dime. A dime was worth something in those days. And here is a perfectly good comb, just needs to be boiled a bit to kill the bugs. Grandmother kept her head high as she walked along; she was a Smith, after all, one of the Smiths. But she never found anything.

SMOKING

Back when I was a kid everyone smoked. My Grandpa smoked cigars, King Edwards. He'd buy them by the box. When the box was empty he'd give me the box. He chewed tobacco as well, Days Work, and he spit into the box of sawdust underneath the table saw. If he'd had the patch and the gum he probably would have done that too. For my dad, it was Lucky Strikes, but he never really had any luck. Uncle Rex, cigars, I think. Uncle Gerald, Old Gold, or maybe it was Chesterfields. Great Uncle Harve smoked a pipe. You'd see him driving down the road in his Ford coupe. He could barely see over the wheel, a short guy, but he smoked a big pipe. He lived into his 90s. While he was in the home, my mother would visit him and try to make him quit smoking. "I can see the burn holes in your pants from that filthy pipe." Uncle Harve took to coloring his leg through each hole with a marking pen so my mother wouldn't notice.

FIRST DAY OF SCHOOL

Goldenrod and tansy are blooming in the ditches, a few of the maple trees are beginning to turn, patches of red here and there among the green, blue sunny skies and white puffy clouds, but the air is cooler today. September. Day after tomorrow is the first day of school. New tennis shoes perhaps, some new pencils and a Big Chief tablet from Vaters' and, if there is change back, penny candy or a licorice flavored wax mustache. Some of the girls will have new dresses. There is an excitement in the air that will be short-lived. Soon the long gray days, the doldrums of the workbook, music lessons and arithmetic. Hours spent staring out the window at row upon row of stratus clouds stretching beyond the horizon, clouds that promise nothing except never to end, and waiting for the bell to ring.

THE LEARNING CURVE

There are certain concepts that I only vaguely understand but that people talk about all the time. You frequently hear the term "learning curve," for instance. I suppose that refers to how one learns a new skill or gains knowledge over a period of time, described as an ascending arc from zero (knowing nothing) to ten, the zenith (knowing all there is to know about a thing). Then comes the gradual descent, the arc of forgetting, back to zero. Then, feet firmly planted on the ground in the batting box of ignorance, the learning curve ball comes whistling past and slowly you come to understand that once again you are out.

SPRING AGAIN

Seagulls sailing close to the wind, clouds running before, everything moving, the waves breaking on some far shore and the water here, all rippled and nervous, the sun stirring the wind which has pushed the ice far out to sea. The sun itself comes spinning in from deep space, the snow melting, pussy willows and catkins, marsh marigolds in the ditch, leaves turning green again, everything wanting and growing. It seems to indicate ... something. But what? Was Aunt Ruth Uncle Karl's sister? What happened to the farm? There is no one to ask. No one and nothing has any more idea what's going on than you do. You are now the resident expert.

AS IS

We've sold the house so we have to move. Now I don't have to think about cutting down that old ugly silver maple tree. I don't have to worry about the squirrels in the attic or mowing the lawn. Not my problem. I intend to blow away like the fluff from a dandelion. One of the last things I'll do before we leave is to drag the old Adirondack chair out to the street corner to be hauled away by anyone who wants it. Sinister device! Sit down there and you may never be able to get up again.

SUPERVISOR

They have knocked down the old school, across the street, bulldozed the little woods nearly out of existence. They are putting up new shops and building affordable housing for students and seniors. All day the trucks and front-end loaders are at work filling the air with dust and noise. I sit and watch as if I were some kind of supervisor. People walk by and say, "How's it going?" "Great," I say. "Right on schedule."

A MAN BUILDS A HOUSE

Once when I was in high school I had a temporary summer job cleaning up around a construction site. The house under construction belonged to a dentist and he was doing a lot of the work himself. Most of the time I was alone on the site but once a day the dentist would drive up in his white pickup truck to check on the progress. One day without even saying hello he said, "I had to divorce my wife the other day. I hated to do it but there wasn't any choice." He said it the way that a man would say he had to shoot his favorite dog. "Really?" I said. On another occasion he said, "You know if we have another war it will be with the English." "Really?" I said. "Yep," he said. "They have been our enemy since 1776. You can't trust those Brits, they want this country back." Then the day I finished up the job he came and paid me off. "Doctor says I've got cancer. I guess I'm going to die." He paused and looked around. "I just hope I can finish this house." I was 17, I didn't know what to say. I still don't.

COULD

Words are very strange. If you look at a word long enough it begins to seem odd. The word, jump, for instance. An odd word to my ear, but I suppose appropriate, juh for the effort of going up and ump for coming down to earth, and it all happens quickly: jump. Other words make less sense to me. "Honey, how do you spell could?" "Could? C-o-u-l-d, why do you ask that?" "Well, that's what I wrote but suddenly it didn't look right." It seems that c-o-u-l-d should be pronounced cold or cooled. But then should would be pronounced shooled and would would be wooled. Could should be spelled c-o-o-d, like good. C-o-u-l-d doesn't look right. Could, meaning the possibility exists. It could happen.

NOTHING IN PARTICULAR

Head bowed, hands folded I may look as if I am saying my prayers, and since I don't really believe in any religion you might say I am saying my prayers to nothing in particular. Or, to put a more positive spin on it, saying my prayers to everything in general, prayers to the chicken house, the freeway, the fading light and the dusty air. If you could see me sitting in my lawn chair on the back porch, it might appear that I have humbled myself before all the phenomena of the earth ... or that I have dozed off again in the late afternoon sun.

WORLDLY GOODS

I've sold or given away most of my books and my tools, and most of my fishing gear and my canoe. I have only one rod and reel left, so some days I sit and fish and some days I just sit. There is a certain satisfaction in the divesting of worldly goods, as there is in quitting a job, a kind of spiritual release, a sanctimony. And every day I feel that I become more godlike, in that soon, like God, I won't do anything at all.

COMPLETE STRANGERS

These days I find it hard to remember which of my contemporaries are dead and which are still alive. But to tell the truth when I meet them on the street or in the grocery store the dead ones don't look that much worse than the living, and none of them has much to say. Mostly, we have found it mutually advantageous to ignore one another, pretending not to see, or that we are complete strangers, and the years pass and eventually we forget entirely. But occasionally there may come one of those awkward moments, at a party or someplace, when our host says, "Art, have you met Elwin?" And there is one of my long dead acquaintances. "Oh, yes I say," shaking Elwin's hand, "we're old friends, we go back a long way." Then, sometime later I wonder, "Now, what was that guy's name?"

WHAT WE MEAN WHEN WE SAY IT'S A BEAUTIFUL DAY

The summer was a disappointment, rain and cold wind. People say, "Last year summer was on a Tuesday, I think. I missed it because I had to work." The garden did not do well. Now it is fall, the leaves bright red, orange and gold in the sunshine, a beautiful day.

Someone says, "Isn't it a nice day?" "Beautiful!" is the proper response. That means the sun is shining, it may be only 20 degrees and the north wind a bit sharp, nevertheless we will not be pushed around. It is a beautiful day.

It means the wind has shifted. It means the snow has stopped falling. It means melt water is running in the street. It means we are still alive. It means the sun is shining and it is a beautiful day.

FIDGET

In my younger days when I had insomnia I would lie awake and worry about things, things in the past that were over, mistakes I had made that were too late to repair. Or I would worry about things to come, difficulties that might never happen. Nowadays I am simply awake, not much to plan for or worry about. So I roll over, scratch, yawn, turn over again, wiggle my toes. The hours go by and I fidget.

SMALL THINGS

Once you stood, brooding, on the cliff overlooking the turbulent sea and the tumultuous clouds, the wind blowing your long hair and the tails of your frock coat. Your role was to make as much noise as possible. Sturm und Drang. But what about the beautiful Marguerite? Ah, forget her ... the world so vast ...

Now your concerns have diminished somewhat. The seas continue to rise, the wind blows, the war goes on. You consider the wing of a bird, a stalk of grass, the late glimmer on the stream surface, realizing that this may be the last time you see any of these things again in this peculiar light. Small things. Like that sliver in the very tip of your finger that despite your best efforts resists removal, so small it is almost invisible, yet when you touch anything, it hurts.

HIDDEN MEANINGS

Once I thought that things had meanings, that perhaps the river flowing, the wind moving a maple branch was a kind of secret signal being sent, a signal, a meaning that always just eluded me. It seemed that if I spread my arms that same wind could carry me into the sky. Now that I am old I happily realize that things and incidents, the bright red leaves tossing in the wind, beautiful as ever on the hillside, the secret world, has no meanings to impart, no hidden messages. But that too, eludes me.

Where Your House Is Now

2019

ELDERLY MAN SHOT AND KILLED BY POLICE

"What shall we do with all these leftover Easter eggs? Make egg salad?" he says.

"I'm tired of egg salad," she says, "besides these are all cracked and dirty from the grandkids playing with them."

"We could throw them at cars," he says.

"That is a great idea!"

"I was kidding," he says.

"No seriously, It will be fun. I bet I can hit more than you."

"We have to try and hit the back of the car so the driver won't be too distracted."

According to a police statement, when the old man raised his hands he appeared to be holding what police thought to be a grenade. The object was later found to be an Easter egg.

The old man's last words to his wife were, "Did you hit any?"

"No," she said.

"Neither did I."

AFTERNOON IN NICE

for Walt Cannon

It must have been France, or Belgium. No it had to be France ... Nice, at a sidewalk café, pigeons walking about under the tables. It was a warm day. Sun. The girls in their summer dresses. I was speaking fluent French and joked with the waiters who responded in French. The problem was that I had no understanding of what they were saying or for that matter, what I was saying, but that has been a problem all along. It all worked out, I guess, because in the end I was served a large bowl of moules et frites and a glass of wine.

TRAVELS

Almost every day I go down to the lakeshore to sit and watch the waves roll in and I am filled with the same old restlessness, the urge to move on ... but where? There is nothing between here and Texas but prairie towns, ethanol plants, and bad Mexican restaurants ... the vagrant dust.

Still, there are places I could go, but where? The Middle East? Definitely not. Not India, China, Russia or Paraguay. Not Antarctica. I once heard of a poet who was awarded a prize, a two-week stay in Antarctica. I think second prize must have been three weeks in Antarctica. I don't want to go to the Amazon, the Congo or any tropical rain forest. In fact in most places there are too many people, and/or other nasty species. I have no desire to see a Komodo dragon or the deadly Irukandji jellyfish. But there was someplace I wanted to go, someplace... I just can't think where right now.

ON KARL JOHAN'S GATE

On Karl Johan's Gate, at a street corner, a man and a woman are arguing in a language I have never heard before. It is a bitter argument. It is possible that they are the only two people in all of Norway who speak this language, they have come a long way, it has been difficult, but they have arrived, at last, on a street corner in Oslo, and now they are lost.

SAVE THE PLANET

It makes no difference to the earth, the earth is fine, carbon dioxide, carbon monoxide, kudzu or tumbleweeds, an abundance of life, or none, life goes on, or not, and it makes no difference to the planet. It's we who care ... or we don't. No more pork belly, no more catfish, no gin at the 18th hole, no more wallowing in the buffalo wallow, no more baby buffalos. No difference. Who cares if Jack manages to buy his chain of car washes? Not me.

GET IT DONE

A lot of heat is produced by the intensity of people trying to get things done. It leads to speeding, tailgating, uneven tire wear, cost overruns, ill considered attire ... The ground is littered with abandoned projects, the telegraph, the Erie Canal... The wheels spin, the grease begins to smoke, the bearings burn up, the wheels fall off and the whole thing is on fire. All the heat produced by this fervor only leads to global warming. Suppose the economy doesn't recover? It's a minor inconvenience. Or a meteor hits the earth? That might cause a lot of initial problems, but in the long run it might do many trillion dollars worth of good.

CULT FOLLOWING

Like most poets my poems never got much attention. They were hardly ever reviewed in literary magazines (which nobody reads anyway) or anywhere, for that matter. But, I still have a few readers scattered here and there, across the country. I like to think of them as a cult following. Perhaps they have a way of recognizing each other, a secret handshake, a wink, a raised eyebrow, whatever ... a group of eccentrics and misfits. I like to imagine that they gather at a designated place deep in the oak forest, at this time of year when the leaves are all nearly down and the moon is full. They build a big bonfire, have a few drinks, read a poem or two of mine aloud, maybe they sing a song, and end by throwing copies of my books into the fire.

AMULET

for Ann

My wife comes to my chair. She is in her nightgown. "Goodnight" she says and gives me a kiss. "Just in case," she adds. I think she means in case I fall asleep before you come to bed. But the possibilities are endless. Just in case the roof falls in from the weight of the snow and we are killed in our beds, or Yellowstone explodes, or suppose America elects a psychopathic moron as president. It is a kind of amulet to protect against illness, pain and poverty; the gathering storm. It's worked (more or less) for us for more than forty years. Just in case, one kiss and goodnight.

DARK MATTER

I just hope that when I die I am really dead. I don't want to be someplace, to be me waiting for something, waiting, sitting in an uncomfortable chair filling out papers. I don't want to meet with a supreme being or this being's amanuensis. I don't want to look from beyond at the ten thousand things, to see things I hate, war, poverty, politicians ... Or the things I like but can no longer have, barbeque ribs, whisky, wind in the trees, birds flying, sunsets across the water, brown paper packages tied up with string, toast and butter ... and of course you, my honey. At most I hope to be a particle, or a part of a particle. Something with no memory, no agenda ... a minor probability.

LIGHTNING

I'm too old and too stupid to write poems anymore. Not that you need to be especially smart to write a poem. You just have to have the knack, to be able to recognize that moment when your hair stands on end, that moment when you are in proximity of lightning. That doesn't occur very often, the time when you get that flash and boom. It hardly ever happens to me anymore. That's for younger people ... Still, I know of several people, around my age, whom I wish would be struck by lightning. Real lightning.

WILL O' THE WISP

There are fewer birds now, an occasional group of fall warblers on their way south. The Hummingbirds disappeared overnight. Patches of yellow here and there in the trees. It is the first day of fall, the season I once thought of as the most beautiful.

At night I stand by the window to try to spot one of those mysterious lights in the swamp down by the river, most often seen during the dark of the moon. Then they vanish. But all I see tonight is the dark reflection of myself in the glass.

SHACK MADE OF STOLEN LINES

I lie long abed in the morning and listen to the barges on the Minnesota River. I lived for many years in the North, amongst the gloom of the tall pines and birches. It was beautiful, but too cold up there for an old man. But I may go back there one day. I know of a hunting shack I can use. It's not much, one room but it has a good cast-iron stove. It has been a late spring. Now mid-May, as I shuffle through the woods, hands in my pockets, a light snow begins to fall. It doesn't really matter, but I may ask myself, "Well, how did I get here?

THOUGHTS GO THROUGH MY HEAD

Thoughts go through my head so swiftly but not as grand or important as lightning, more like static electricity, when your hair stands up for no reason, except dry air maybe, little tiny ideas, or the remnants of ideas, something like little blind kittens that will soon be drowned. The last thing I need, anyway, is more cats.

The Mad Moonlight

2019

WINTER EVENING

As we get older we become more alone.
The man and his wife share this gift.
They make love or they quarrel.
They move through the day,
she on the black squares,
he on the white.
At night they sit by the fire,
he reading his book, she knitting.
The fire is agitated.
The wind hoots in the chimney like a child
blowing in a bottle,
happily.

SAUNA

Even to step naked
into the January night is a pleasure!
Steam rises from our bodies
and forms high, thin clouds
that go racing past the moon over the lake.

HERE IT IS MARCH

This winter has been going on for eleven years.
It's amazing how one gets concerned
with other things
and the time just goes by.
Here it is March
and now that I've noticed it,
the snow has begun to melt a little.
During the day there's water
running in the street.
It's like a bird singing in a tree
that flies just as you become aware of it.
When you think about it, the world,
cold and hard as it is,
begins to fall apart.

I USED TO

When I got older I used to like
To sit and watch the young women go by,
especially in summer.
That's all I did, watch.
All I could do, really.
Now that I am even older
and my eyesight fails,
I find I can't really see the girls.
Just a blurred memory.

CHEKHOV AND HEISENBERG

I tell my brother-in-law
that we stayed in the hotel where
Chekhov had stayed, in Nice.
He tells me that he once stayed
in the very hotel room that
Werner Heisenberg
had occupied back in 1926.
He thought the hotel was either
in Copenhagen or maybe Leipzig...
But he was uncertain.

APPENDAGE POEM

Every time I look for money
I find a hand in my pocket.

UNIVERSE

Sometimes I think that I am the universe.
Take a look at my bare back;
spots and stars, galaxies,
nebulae, bumps, dark matter, super nova ...
But it is all just skin-deep.

SAGES IN SPRING

As soon as the snow melts
the grass begins to grow,
even though the daytime high
is barely above freezing.
May is very like November.
Popple trees produce a faint green
that hangs under the low clouds
like a haze over the valley.
This is how the sages live, no complaints,
no suspicion, no surprise.
If it rains carry an umbrella.
If it's cold wear a jacket.

BIRTHDAY

It's my birthday.
Well, every day is someone's birthday;
think of that … many people's birthday,
over 300,000 birthdays every day.
And if today is your birthday,
remember, nobody gives a shit.
Just blow out the candles on your cake
if you are lucky enough to have one.

BREAD UPON THE WATERS

As quickly as that,
in that moment your attention focused
somewhere far out there,
on the bit of sun brightening the surface,
the baby drifted away,
his diaper changed, his bottle filled,
he rides the waves in his basket, like a king,
a bit uncomfortable, and slightly annoyed.

THREE DAY RAIN

It has been raining for three days,
a slow unrelenting rain,
east wind, 43 degrees;
an average day in June.
Everything is soggy and rotting.
Earth worms are drowning.
We have no money, nowhere to go.
The gray goose stands in the yard
with her head under her wing.

RENT FREE

I don't get around very well anymore.
I'm unsteady on my feet.
I can't sit in a canoe anymore.
It hurts my back.
I have trouble sleeping.
My speech is sometimes garbled.
Reading is difficult; no ability to concentrate.
My feet hurt, and I have very low energy.
So these days I live mostly in my head.
You could live there too,
if you need a temporary place to stay.
It's quiet, And there's lots of room.

DREAM OF WEALTH

The stars are neither large
nor very distant.
They are made of delicate glass
imported from Sweden and sold
at a huge profit.

GREEN SNAKE

There is a green snake
moving in and out of our conversation.
Hungry, he eats the dots of the j's and the i's.
We grope blindly for words.

PHYSICAL THERAPY

Because I am feeling pretty good today,
I say to my therapist
I think I'll live, at least, five more years.
She says, "You think?"

THERE IS NO GOD IN HEAVEN

There is no God in heaven
who thinks you are special
the way your mother did.
The earth does not think
you are more special
than any centipede or rat.
The earth is not your mother,
and heaven is not your home.

THE RUNNER

She has long legs and short shorts.
She wears her long blond hair
tied in a neat bun. Each move she makes
is perfect, not too fast, not too slow.
She glides along down the sidewalk,
leaving me breathless,
A block away the sidewalk curves
and she is gone forever.

ARMCHAIR

I have a large comfortable swivel armchair.
And if I turn it one way
I can see the large-screen TV, and
if I turn the opposite
I can watch the colorful birds
at the feeder.
I suppose it would be more correct to say
that I prefer the birds, but in truth,
I view them both about the same.
Of the things in this poem
I like the armchair best.

THE WOLF

Where are we going now? I ask
the wolf, as he struggles
to drag my carcass across the snow.
But the wolf does not answer, knowing
it is impolite to speak
with your mouth full.

OLD PEOPLE

Some people live too long,
they get foggy and grouchy,
they smell, they sleep and snore,
and pee their pants.
No one really likes old people,
they are in the way. Worst of all
is that they contribute nothing
to the current mass hallucination.

SUMMER RAIN

Lightning strikes. The clock stops.
The voice on the radio fades.
We sit in the dark living room as in a cave,
without light, without words.

The rain continues to fall all night.
We sleep and drift among roads, houses
and people we have known. I wake and listen,
the sound of rain, the sound of our breathing.
Water rising.

LITERARY SILLINESS

Johnny Cash sang
I don't care if I do die do die do die.
And Aeneas once said
I don't care for Dido Dido Dido.
As did WS Merwin.

GUILTY

I went down to the Sheriff's Department
and said "I'm here to turn myself in."
"Indeed?" said the deputy.
"And what crime have you committed?"
"I was hoping you could tell me that," I said.

MORNING FOG

I know I'll get back to sleep
when the morning fog comes in,
when the Pacific fleet arrives,
ghost ships from the Coral Sea.
They never cough or shuffle their feet
but I know they're in the room,
great hulking shapes, old
and unpleasant relatives,
the color of the sea, the color of the sky,
gathered around my bed.

WIND FROM THE WEST

It isn't so much because of the desire
for what has been lost,
as it is the loss of desire itself,
that I stand here, on the verge of tears.
like a child, whose big red ball
has washed out to sea.

TEETH

Once you leave the river,
once you start up the long valley
you catch the first glimpse
of mountains snow-capped
sharp white in the distance.
When they see you, smile.

PLEASURE DRIVE

I used to drive most of the time.
But old age caught up to me. Now
my wife does most of the driving.
I've discovered that I like being a passenger.
I have time to look out the window
and at the people,
the trees, the buildings, and the clouds above.
My wife likes it too.
She's honed her skills at moving through traffic,
and she is not opposed to speed now and then.
We strap on our seat belts, she hums sotto voce to herself.
It's "The Ride of the Valkyries," I think.
And away we go like a bat outta hell.

THOUGHTBERRIES

So called because once you spend a
day picking, you will think twice
about ever doing it again.
Thoughtberries are not plentiful,
picking the low stickery bushes
to gather just a handful.
Their scarcity must be part of their appeal
because, really, they aren't all that good.
There are not enough of them in these parts
to make them a commercially viable product,
but then in many parts of the country
they don't grow at all.

YOUTH

One hand holding up
his oversize trousers,
the other clutching a burger,
he races across the street
just ahead of the oncoming traffic.

WHAT IF

I were to die just before
the announcement was made
that I had won the Pulitzer Prize,
or the National Book Award,
or Poet Lariat of the United States,
and the irony of that
were to be entirely lost on me?

WITCHES

Young witches
The young witches love to dance
at night in the moonlight, wearing their very
skimpy black dresses.
And the big handsome boys
come down from town.
The girls lead them through the forest,
down the darkened paths.
And the boys get turned
around and lost.
Those boys are dumber than sticks, thick as bricks, and
those girls are *wick-ed*.

Old witches
The old witches live in huts deep in the forest.
They know the secret of wolfsbane, snakeroot
plants and herbs,
which are poison and which will make you well.
They make elixirs, potions and poultices,
balm for heartbreak, remorse, disillusionment,
for all the pains of old age and death ...
Good luck to you, if you can find them.

KNOCK KNOCK

A large woodpecker is at work
on the wood shingles of my house,
making a terrible racket ...
looking for grubs and worms.
He has a different agenda, his own
viewpoint, his own facts,
a separate reality.
I, myself, would never even think of
pecking on a roof.

TONIGHT THE FULL MOON

Rises above Lake Superior,
All sad and luminous.
and filling me with joy. How many times
have clouds obscured the sky
in the last fifty years?
And how many times have I been
lucky enough to see the moonrise like this?

TO THE MUSE

All the years I spent waiting for you
to come to me here on this shore,
rehearsing what we would say to one another
and the happiness that would be ours.
Now that I am old, it occurs to me
that you must have come,
but I was too distracted to see you there.

FOLK TALE

Times were tough so we decided
to sell the cow.
I walked the long road into town
leading the cow.
But no one was buying.
On the way home I met a man
who had a horse.
So we swapped. I met others. I swapped
the horse for a pig, the pig for a sheep,
the sheep for a goat, and so on until
I came home with nothing.
But I was born lucky and
the best part of my luck was that
you stood by me
through all the blundering mistakes.
One time I had a windfall.
We were able to buy a new cow ...
Which means I'll soon be
on the road again.

BRIGHTON BEACH WAVES

White-haired but determined,
as if each had a purpose, a private destiny,
someplace to go.
Once the savior walked across the water
to give each wave a hand up.
Perhaps he is returning even now,
but the road to the shore is long, long ...
The waves break and fall face forward,
losing touch, losing credibility,
losing all pretense of dignity.

LAKE SUPERIOR

What I like best
are those rocks that
for no apparent reason
stand waist-deep
in the water and refuse
to come into shore.

Fragments from the Notebooks, Unpublished and Early Drafts

The Boundary Waters

Night has come again
the fire has burned down
to a few scattered ~~to~~ cools
that glow like the eyes of animals.
And so I lie down to sleep
on the ground.
Behind my head
the wilderness stretches all the way
to the arctic tundra, to the North Sea,
to the Aurora Borealis.
It belongs to the night creatures
the owl, the wolf,
the moose browsing in the cedar swamp.
I'm not used to this life.
I ache from the hard portages,
the days on the water,
the sun and wind.
The earth is hard
and for awhile fear holds me
stiff against it.
But, at last,
that too drains away into ~~sleep~~,
~~to~~ the damp roots and stones.
This is the boundary waters
of the last sleep with Dreams.
When it has gone
our lives will be a buzz of light,
brief and constant,
until the oldest darkness
comes back again.

FRAGMENTS

Louis Jenkins' handwritten notebooks can be found in the collections of the University of Minnesota Libraries, Archives and Special Collections, Upper Midwest Literary Archives. The following are selections from those notebooks, sometimes only beginning sentences or ideas, incomplete poems, and complete but unpublished work. The order here is random, not chronological, perhaps appropriate as he would often return to an unfinished poem many years later to try to complete the piece.

※

… Here in the north, there is no spring really. The cold lingers well into April, decides to go, packs, changes its mind, unpacks, hesitates until one day, with no warning, it's summer. Suddenly the trees have leaves, flowers are in bloom, vegetation falling over itself to grow quickly before the cold changes its mind again. It's warm and sunny with a slight breeze from the south, a few stately white clouds drifting by like parade floats. Summer is here, like a surprise party. One has mixed feelings. Here are your friends and relatives, all your old girlfriends. Everywhere the young pressing around, tall and slender grasses whispering, deferent. You are the guest of honor after all.

… Last night's dream wants to reclaim you when you lie down. Like an old lover who pleads and cries, but really has lost interest in the affair.

In the middle ages they believed in heaven and clung to the earth even though beaten senseless until someone hacheted their finger away..

... The danger might be only a rattling in the popple leaves, a shadow darkening this place which is nowhere, just some rocks, a possibility of falling. The danger is all you are, some shifting moods, could be that's all you are ...

... Economics – He shuffles some paper, so do you, move things from place to place, more zeroes in his column. Buy some gas, you give them one bill, they give you back four, but they're not worth as much as your original one, he's got gas, ...we are all on our way again...

... There are things for which there is no remedy, that no amount of education or good will can help...

... Our reaction is instinctive danger overhead – freeze where you are – as in the statue game? It's nothing, sunlight and shadow, the clouds going overhead like a passing thought...

... Someone who has passed on says, if there's any way, I'll come back. I'll get a message to you. There was nothing, of course, only the sky, the sunset day after day that seemed to promise something, but there was nothing. She knew. Perhaps you just can't hear the voice ... the vastness contains nothing ...

... Finally one lives beyond reason, beyond the muck of real life, on the barest of threads, beyond hope, beyond idea in the high, bright rarified air ...

... You always imagine yourself at the center of life, at the center of your own life. It's difficult to imagine that this is your real life, right now, thinking about a sandwich and a beer.

... Where I live in Northern Minnesota, we don't have long summers. Thunderstorms don't amount to much really, not like farther out on the plains where the light turns violet or green and there's hail the size of baseballs, and tornadoes. We don't have poisonous snakes or very much violent crime. People are polite if a bit distant. We don't even have that much snow really, compared to Northern Michigan, or the mountains. What we have is cold, 60 below. Cold, even in the summer, it lingers. If you put your hand way to the back of a cupboard, you can feel it grab your wrist, you can feel its breath rising from the lake in the morning. But the cold, though often it may seem otherwise, is only another absence.

... Sometimes the dead are given a second chance, the boat is filled and pulls away leaving one lonely soul on the shore. The pennies lifted from his eyes. He reappears on the street somewhat dazed and distracted, like someone whose luggage has been flown to Cleveland by accident. He seems unsteady in a strange city.

... Artists and Intellectuals, they are named in the same breath, as if they had something in common, sometimes artists pretend to be intellectuals and vice versa, but usually not at the same party. An intellectual talks and nobody knows what it means.

... Jewelry, watches, cameras, accessories, but where will you find the true gift? Will you know it? There must be a half a dozen gift shops between here and Two Harbors alone. Even if you drive to the dead end of the loneliest back road, there's a sign saying gifts–antiques. And what if it's not quite right? Well, if it cost an arm and a leg, it's a stop on your quest ...

… without a compass or a map, I crossed and recrossed
my own trail, all the trees, all the landmarks remarkably
similar, a heavy overcast blocked the sun and in late
afternoon a light rain began to fall. At dusk I stumbled
and rolled into a small ravine. I crawled under the low
hanging branches of a big spruce tree for shelter, and sat
there all night rocking back and forth, crying…

… In the yellow light of the room you brush out your
hair and I lie still on the bed.

"What can we do?" I ask. There is no answer, and when
the light is turned out it is so dark I can't see my hand in
front of my face, but it is you I reach out to, no other.

UNPUBLISHED POEMS AND EARLY DRAFTS

Picnic on the Shore (first draft)

Tufts of grass growing
from the cracks of the big rocks
deeply rooted
enduring year after year.
This is the way you want to live
a simple life
the proper ordering of a few elements

but, here you are
trying to balance a plate
and cup while standing
on slippery stone
What with the wind and the flies
Already things have gotten out of hand.

Fall

The trees blaze up red and gold
And you are afraid of that fire.
Which light among all the others is yours?
What is it that you wait for every day?
What is it that you look for
among the fallen leaves?
Some mornings the fog comes in off the water
and each thing is alone,
concerned with itself.
And if at night you do not fall immediately asleep
you may see that even your left hand
lies away from you,
dreaming,
like a dog near the fire,
something you have forgotten
or never knew.

The Glacier

The small sounds
a book falling against another on the shelf
or the silverware shifting in the drawer
only increase the silence,
and the ice surrounds you
white as far as you can see
cut with deep crevasses
(everyone knows stories of those who have vanished)
It holds you near the sun
And the incredible blue sky
while it moves
imperceptibly
to the sea.

Mosquitoes

They have a blood lineage
more ancient than the Pharoahs
a purity your life has ever known,
a singularity of purpose
that does not exhaust itself
before death.
Their constant drone has no meaning,
it is the sound of the wilderness itself
surrounding the tent.
Their weight is a constant pressure
more persistent than memory or sleep.
A stake pulls free.
One side of the tent sags.
They find the smallest opening.

Winter Night

Tonight cold and silence
Have returned to each other.
It is useless to pretend that
nothing has changed.
Doors that once opened at a touch
refuse to move
and machinery, whose friendship
you so casually assumed,
won't work and is dangerous
to touch barehanded.
Everything that once seemed so alive
is immobile and dumb.
But something stirs.
A yawn in the beams beneath the floor
startles you.
What was it?

There is no wind
and smoke from the chimney
for a moment assumes
the shape of someone safely forgotten,
then changes and moves away
from your ordinary sleeping house
across the road
and vanishes
in the frozen trees.

December (first draft)

The days are short
each one a splinter of light
like a note on white paper
shoved under the door
of a dark apartment.
"I need 300 dollars right away."

How good it is at night
to walk away from the noise,
into the trees and listen
to the snow falling,
covering the tracks of the day.
It is a song the dead sing,
so uneasy in our frightening world.

Fog

Fog comes in suddenly from the lake
some trouble that has been growing
a long time in secret.
An accident, an illness,
a telephone call, a message
that someone's heart has stopped
as suddenly as a power mower

that has run over a chain.
Lights going on in a house
well past midnight.
Far out on the water a ship's horn sounds.
Fog comes in and each thing is surrounded,
isolated, concerned with itself.
I want to say all this brings us closer
and I reach out to touch you
sleeping nearby in the dark.
I know that something has found
shelter for the night
in those wet hulking pines outside the window
those massive black shapes
at the edge of the visible world.

Florida (first draft)

A pretty girl passes wearing a T-shirt with FLORIDA
printed across the front in orange letters, and I can't
help it, I think of citrus fruit. I think of Cubans tending
smudge pots in the groves. Night and stars. Wallace
Stevens walking on the beach at Key West wearing a
white suit. And everything green. Insects everywhere,
and flamingos. Snakes hanging from every tree and
alligators sunning themselves on the banks of the river.
Such long hot days and humid nights. Nothing to do
but lie around the shack and fish these languid, sinister
waters. Oh, but what's to become of our love? We've
let things slide. The weeds grow higher, the swamp gets
closer. There's less and less to say, less difference between
day and night. The rent is unpaid. One day the real estate
man will come driving up in his DeSoto. He has plans for
this place.

The Lighthouse (first draft)

The light flashes across the water and is gone, the way
headlights of a car turning the corner cross the walls
of a dark room where someone is awake all night. It all
happens so quickly, no way to take back the things that
were said. Your son drove headlong into a train. Your
daughter is in a Mexican jail. The flash of light is like a
house passed at 80 miles per hour. Did anyone live there?
Were they asleep? The night, the sea, the wind and the
rocks. The terrible current off shore. It is so good to see
the light across the water. It is a warning, this is the place
where the water ends and the land begins. Either way is
dangerous. It is there we must live, the only possibility. It
is that light we rush toward, that we call home.

Poem for This House

No matter how we packed
repacked, painted, and plastered
Or what pain we brought
to go on living with us
like an ancient spinster aunt.
This house has its own dark wood
its breath, water, and stone.
Sleep surrounding us
as the forest
and I love to see you
stirred awake at dawn
moving in its shadow
or silhouetted a moment
against the eastern window.

Lakeshore (for Robert Bly)

Water washes up on the flat stone, up nearly to the edge
and back, then up again, farther and finally over into a
small pool that overflows, back to the main body. The
surface of the rock is slick, covered with algae that needs
only water and sunlight. It is possible to live here, to
marry, make friends, and have children. The motion of
water, constant for centuries reaching out, smoothing,
diminishing, returning.

When the wind was high from the northeast, water
splashed up into this little hollow on the top of a big
rock and stayed like the family whose covered wagon
broke down in Kansas on the way to the West Coast.
Now, molecule by molecule this water is ascending. The
water vanishes on a hot day but will return at night,
rain far out on the lake, a rumbling in your dreams, the
covers twisted around your feet.

My Grandparents Farm

My grandparents farm is no more now than a hole in the
ground surrounded by lilacs and mulberry trees. The
house, the barn, the outbuildings were moved away or
torn down more that twenty years ago. The debris around
the place is vaguely familiar, like an old idea used again
in a poem. The lives of my grandparents and my great
grandparents are remarkable only for their distance, not
even any earthy stories remain. What I know of them is
only fragments, like bits of a dream recalled. And, when
in dreams, members of my family and friends appear, the
living come along with the dead and the disremembered.
No one is surprised. They speak to me of concerns that
are different from those expressed during waking hours.
This leads me to believe I'm never getting the complete

picture. The fragments surround me like iron filings around a magnet. A circle dance, day and night. The life surrounds me and moves outward like the petals of a flower from the dark center. I stand on the rock, the sun shines, the wind rises, the waves rush in and break at my feet. The light is shattered in a million pieces.

A Wedding Gift for Michael and Lisa

A new car would be nice. Something special. An event of this magnitude requires something excessive. A Rolls-Royce in silver or powder blue, leather interior, stereo, maybe a TV, liquor cabinet...champagne on ice! And a chauffeur, of course. I can see him with his uniform, cap, neat little mustache, walking slowly round and round the Rolls (which is parked outside the Willard Motel and Coffee Shop), wiping a spot of dust here and there, tapping a tire with the toe of a shiny black boot, glancing at his watch ... no, that isn't quite right. Perhaps a Mercedes or even a used Volvo. Times being what they are I can barely manage an occasional evening at the local bar or an occasional poem. When I look around my poetry and automobile repair shop, I see a discarded crankcase, a few carburetors, various cast-off parts ...here is a '60 Chevy with no rear end. That won't do. The automobile is a complicated mechanical and metaphorical device. For this journey you need something tough, inexpensive to operate and easily repaired. Now over in the back lot I have a Dodge pickup that might be just the thing. It needs paint, the tires are fair, plenty of room for the dogs and a case of beer in back. No Rolls-Royce certainly, but I can tell from your faces today that it doesn't matter. Here's the road, trees on either side, perhaps a bird or two, the lake below the hill, the sun coming up or going down, the moon rising ...

See Saw

At the very heart of the forest
is a huge grey stone,
worn smooth by the last
glacier to pass this way.
It seems that such a simple thing
ought to hold a simple answer,
and it does: same thing
on the inside as on the out.
Only a blind thing,
a root or a man would bother
breaking open a stone.
No need.
Just place a plank across the top,
you sit on one end,
your love on the other.
Up and down, up and
own, the elemental mystery.
Top o' the world,
like the North Pole,
every direction from here
is the direction you came from,
yet nothing you see
going down looks like
anything you saw coming up.

The Boundary Waters

Night has come again,
the fire has burned down
to a few scattered coals
that glow like the eyes of animals.
And so I lie down to sleep

on the ground.
Behind my head
the wilderness stretches all the way
the the arctic tundra, to the North Sea,
to the Aurora Borealis.
It belongs to the night creatures,
the owl, the wolf,
the moose browsing in the cedar swamp.
I'm not used to this life.
I ache from the hard portages,
the days on the water,
the sun and wind.
The earth is hard
and for a while fear holds me
stiff against it.
But, at last
that too drains away into
the damp roots and stones.
This is the boundary waters
of the last sleep with dreams.
When it has gone
our lives will be a buzz of light,
brief and constant,
until the oldest darkness
comes back again.

October Forecast

The weather forecast predicts no Indian summer
days – just the long grim slide into winter, snow
flurries and cold. Outside I can't tell if it is the
wind in the eaves or a distant siren that makes
such a mournful sound.

The Artist's House
(For Joy and Lyle)

The artist built himself a house in the woods. He did
not know how to build and he was too stubborn to take
advice, except what he overheard and usually got wrong.
His house was cribbled together from whatever he could
find, old bricks and boards, logs he cut in the woods.
It was never quite right, but it stood. Then one day the
artist sold a painting. With some of the money he bought
an old pickup from a neighbor. He drove to town and
bought new paper and paint to make more pictures. He
bought groceries and a lot of beer. On the way home he
hit a boulder in the road, tore open the oil pan, lost all the
oil and seized up the engine of his truck. He had to walk
home carrying the groceries and the beer, but he forgot
the paper in the back of the pickup. Then it began to rain.
When he got home, soaking wet, he found a note saying
that his wife had left him. "Never mind," he thought,
"I'll have a party." So, he invited all his neighbors and all
his crazy artist friends to a big barbecue and they partied
all night long. When the artist woke next afternoon,
everyone had gone, the place was a mess, and his last
five dollars was missing. But, he was well off indeed. His
house was surrounded by a circle of popple trees. The sky
covered his estate and the entire earth enclosed it.

Matters of Substance

One wearies of matters of substance.
I recommend those moments that,
without reason, last a lifetime:
the red-haired girl on the shore
brushing her teeth as we sailed away,
the glimpse of a face, a shoulder in a doorway;
moments like music, truth untroubled by meaning.

(Untitled)

I am so drunk
that my wife has to drive.
What a beautiful night!
wind and moon shining
through the fast moving clouds.
When I get home I will turn the dogs loose
to run wild all night.

(Untitled)

When the thunder starts
and the wind gusts
you come into our bed.
I enjoy this summer storm
and you don't mind it now
still small enough to nestle
in on my leaside away
from the window, the wind.
But, each day more complex explanations are required,
you learn words easily.

BOOKS BY LOUIS JENKINS

The Well Digger's Wife (Morris, MN: Minnesota Writers' Publishing House, 1973)

The Wrong Tree: Thirteen Prose Poems (Stevens Point, WI: Scopcraeft Press, 1980)

The Water's Easy Reach (Buffalo, NY: White Pine Press, 1985)

An Almost Human Gesture (St. Paul, MN: Eighties Press & Ally Press, 1987)

All Tangled Up with the Living (St. Paul, MN: Nineties Press, 1991)

Nice Fish: New and Selected Prose Poems (Duluth, MN: Holy Cow! Press, 1995)

Just Above Water (Duluth, MN: Holy Cow! Press, 1997)

The Winter Road (Duluth, MN: Holy Cow! Press, 2000)

Sea Smoke (Duluth, MN: Holy Cow! Press, 2004)

Distance from the Sun (Minneapolis, MN: Minnesota Center for Book Arts, 2004)

Four Places on Lake Superior's North Shore (Red Wing, MN: Red Dragonfly Press, 2005)

Fisk på tørt land: prosadikt (Trondheim, Norway: pir forlag, 2007)

North of the Cities (Duluth, MN: Will o' the Wisp Books, 2007)

European Shoes (Duluth, MN: Will o' the Wisp Books, 2008)

Before You Know It: Prose Poems 1970-2005 (Duluth, MN: Will o' the Wisp Books, 2009)

Tin Flag: New and Selected Prose Poems (Duluth, MN: Will o' the Wisp Books, 2013)

In the Sun Out of the Wind (Bloomington, MN: Will o' the Wisp Books, 2017)

Where Your House Is Now: New and Selected Prose Poems, (Minneapolis: Nodin Press, 2019)

The Mad Moonlight (Bloomington, MN: Will o' the Wisp Books, 2019)

BY LOUIS JENKINS AND RICHARD C. JOHNSON

Words and Pictures (Duluth, MN: Will o' the Wisp Books, 2012)

BY MARK RYLANCE AND LOUIS JENKINS

Nice Fish: A Play (New York, NY: Grove Press, 2017)

Index

Note: Early drafts and unpublished poems appear in italics.

ABOUT THE AUTHOR

Louis Jenkins' poems have appeared in numerous literary magazines and anthologies. He has published nineteen collections of poetry. He was awarded two Bush Foundation Fellowships for poetry, a Loft-McKnight fellowship, and was the recipient of the 2000 George Morrison Award. Mr. Jenkins has read his poetry on *A Prairie Home Companion* and was a featured poet at the Geraldine R. Dodge Poetry Festival in 1996 and at the Aldeburgh Poetry Festival, Aldeburgh, England in 2007.

Beginning in 2008, Louis Jenkins and Mark Rylance, Academy Award-winning actor and former director of the Globe Theatre, London, began work on a stage production titled *Nice Fish*, based on Mr. Jenkins' poems. The play premiered April 6, 2013, at the Guthrie Theater in Minneapolis and ran through May 18 of that year. A revised version of the play had runs at American Repertory Theater in Boston, St. Ann's Warehouse in New York City, and The Harold Pinter Theatre in London's West End. In March 2017 *Nice Fish* was nominated for an Olivier Award as Best New Comedy of 2017.

Printed in the USA
CPSIA information can be obtained
at www.ICGtesting.com
JSHW021900081023
49707JS00004B/9/J